SHAFTED

Cautionary Tales in Business

Ken H. Delmar

Ken H. Delmar
Visit my website at www.KenDelmarAuthor.com

Printed in the United States of America

First Printing: 02-08-2020
Amazon KDP

ISBN-978-1-7344885-4-8

"To be prepared is half the victory"
MIGUEL DE CERVANTES SAAVEDRA

"The boy who is going to make a great man
must not make up his mind merely to overcome
a thousand obstacles, but to win in spite of a
thousand repulses and defeats."
THEODORE
ROOSEVELT

Forewarned Is Forearmed
MOTTO OF THE US ARMY SECURITY AGENCY

For my wife, Ulli, who has always been my steady and resilient first mate through thunderously thick and terrifyingly thin.

INTRODUCTION

Shafted, Cautionary Tales in Business is for people starting out, starting a business, intending to grow a business, taking an MBA, or who have taken an MBA and sensed that something was missing. It's also for people who are studying business law, or who mean to practice law and need to arm themselves with examples from real life of how devious and mean-spirited human nature in pursuit of profit and power can be.

Most of us like to read uplifting, positive, inspirational stories with happy endings. *Chicken Soup for the Soul* is a very successful self-help, media, and consumer goods company that exploded out of our need for inspiration, encouragement, and silver linings in a real world that isn't always cheerful, treacly, positive and uplifting. Chicken Soup stories are an ongoing venture, and new editions are published regularly. If you are looking for a relief from reality, a rose-colored view of the world, blithe inspiration, and happy endings, there are plenty of books, videos, podcasts, audio books, movies, podcasts, plays, musicals, blogs and programs to accommodate you and cheer you up.

Shafted does not fall into this genre. It will not cheer you up, put a tear on your cheek, restore your faith in human nature, or give you goose-bumps. It will, more likely, piss you off and make you angry and irritable for the rest of the day, if not the week. *Shafted* offers you the other side of the coin; un-sweetened, dismayingly true, unleavened stories from real life that spin out of raw, ambitious, aggressive human nature. It is going to rip off the rose-colored glasses and expose the egregious behavior generated by the mean-spirited, pernicious, selfish, arrogant, insidious and greedy side of human behavior. Shafted is the antidote to Chicken Soup.

The premise of *Shafted* was first recorded in the Ancient Greek and Roman Empires as the proverb, "Praemonitus, praemunitus," or "Forewarned is forearmed." But it probably goes back even further, to the earliest clans and communities of Neanderthal and other archaic homo sapiens of Eurasia, who were, no doubt, subject to the earliest iterations of human nature, which even then must have enabled those who were forewarned and forearmed to anticipate, survive, and ultimately -- prevail.

YOUR DUTCH UNCLE

"What's a Dutch Uncle?" asked my daughter, Alex. "I don't know what that is, and if I don't know what it is, no one does." Alex, forty-something, (I had her when I was twelve) is very well-read, and very much in touch, and she's absolutely right. So here's the definition:

A Dutch uncle, or aunt, is a person, wise in the ways of the world, who has been there and done that, who cares enough about you to tell you cautionary tales, give you pragmatic advice and warnings, un-sugar-coated and raw, to prepare you for bumps, potholes and hairpin turns in the road ahead. Your parents and grandparents, if you are lucky enough to have such relatives, spend a ton of love and time and money sheltering you from reality for as long as they can, from the bruises and betrayals, disappointments and losses, snakes and rats lurking in the path ahead. When the time comes, when he or she thinks you are ready, your Dutch uncle or aunt takes off your warm and fuzzy rose-coloured glasses and replaces them with clear, unfiltered, vision.

When you're working towards a goal, initiating a project, striving to prevail in a competitive environment, delivering on promises, doing your duty, following your muse, or laying in the gutter with the wind kicked out of you by the pointy-toed boot of ruthless reality; when you are a broker, dealer, entrepreneur, inventor, job candidate, salesperson, or you are trying to start a business, offer a service, sell or promote something, raise money, lead a team or drive a campaign, you could really use a Dutch uncle to caution you up front about the obstacles and bad behavior you are most likely to encounter; a Dutch uncle who will help prevent you from being shafted, exploited, manipulated, hoodwinked, betrayed, lead down the primrose path, sold a bill of goods, or thrown under the bus. A Dutch uncle who will help you pick yourself up, dust yourself off, and start all over again.

If you don't have a Dutch uncle or aunt, don't despair, I am happy to take the role for you in *Shafted*. I will identify for you the roadblocks, detours and obstacles that villains, false friends, con artists, liars, haters and competitors will inevitably interpose between you and your goals.

I will rejoice with you when you recognize ulterior agendas, traitors, liars and cheats early on and use that knowledge to convert potential losses to wins. I will fly with you when you rise from the wounds of combat undaunted and ready to meet the next challenge wiser, stronger, and better armed to win.

I have restricted myself to tales in which I was a primary player, or got the story live and straight from the horse's mouth and other reliable sources as it unfolded. When necessary, I have changed names to avoid a frivolous lawsuit, or broken windows in the middle of the night. I have told 24 tales here as a tribute to Chaucer's Canterbury Tales. Chaucer intended to write 120 tales, but he died upon finishing 24. Ooops. I hope that's not a harbinger of my fate!

Shafted, Cautionary Tales in Business will make you better prepared for setbacks and disappointments, because you will be ready for them, and you will confidently work your way past them to the clear sailing and new opportunities on the other side.

CONTENTS

CHAPTER 1 IT'S ONLY BUSINESS, DON'T TAKE IT PERSONALLY

About six months after I started a film production company in Manhattan in the early seventies, I got a lead on a piece of business at ITT WorldCom, a major communications company. They wanted to have a film made that would show all their present and prospective customers that communications would be faster from now on, because all their old electro-mechanical switches were being replaced with fully electronic ones. I proposed a *Mission Impossible* theme, wrote a script for their approval, and they gave me the green light to start work on the film.

Part of the project was to distribute to some 130 ITT sales and marketing offices around the world a looped (endless play) Super-8 print of the film and a portable projector unit, with which their field people could show the film to customers and potential customers. At the time, the state-of-the-art projectors were made by the Fairchild Company. These units were convertible to either front or rear projection onto a captive screen about fifteen inches square. Another popular unit, lighter and less expensive, but perhaps not quite as reliable, was offered by the Bohn-Benton company.

My client at ITT asked me to bid on delivering a number of these units along with the film. The order was for 100 of the Fairchild Projectors and 30 of the Bohn-Bentons. I went to Fairchild and told them I wanted to become a dealer, and already had a customer that was ready to buy. They said I had to buy at least one model of each projector in their line before I could become a dealer. Same story at Bohn-Benton. I said fine. I bought two projectors from Fairchild, and one from B-B (the only model they had), and became a dealer for both companies. The Fairchild units retailed for around $450 each, and wholesaled at around $200. For the 100 Fairchilds, I was going to make $25,000.00. The Bohn-Bentons listed at around $300 each, and wholesaled at around $150, something like that, so on them I would make $4,500.

For being a dealer and delivering 130 projectors I was going to make an incredible $29,500. For a commercial/industrial filmmaker, who has to earn every wretched cent he makes, this was astonishing. My wife couldn't believe it; she made me do the math again and again. She kept asking, "And all you have to do is order these things, load in the film cassette, test run them, and deliver them to ITT?" Yes – that was it! It was that simple. It was just business, how business is done.

Business was great... I loved business. I, a writer and artist, was ready to walk away from everything I knew and loved, and become a crass philistine businessman! This was all new and exciting to me, because I knew very little about business and

8

businesspeople. My dad was an actor and comedian and my mother a ballerina and artist. There was no talk of business or businesspeople, except perhaps to disparage them as creatively deficient, culturally Neanderthal, materialistic and bourgeois. From my mother's pre-bellum-southern-lady perspective, anyone who engaged in business was some sort of wretched merchant, and by definition of a lower class – it was irrelevant how much money they had amassed being a wretched merchant.

From my father's point of view, businesspeople were squares and drones who had voluntarily committed themselves to a miserable 9:00 to 5:00 hell of quiet desperation. And here I was, with my first revelation of what attracts those drone-like materialists; a fast and healthy profit for doing very little indeed -- buying and selling stuff; being the middleman; wallowing in a flood of unwarranted gains. I could get into this!

I sent my client the numbers he needed for his purchase order, and offered a discount of ten percent for the Fairchild order, since it was for a hundred units. My client went over the figures on the phone with me and asked for my assurance that the Fairchild units would be the very latest model, which I had shown him before I had to return it to my distributor. Oh, sure, I said, absolutely. He said to watch the mail for his purchase order. It was very important to him that I deliver at least one of these new models to the big upcoming sales meeting in Hawaii, three weeks hence, so that he could demo it to all the salespeople in the audience. I told him that I would make that happen.

I called my Fairchild distributor to ask him if he could loan me one of the brand new super-duper models for my client's Hawaii sales meeting, careful not to reveal the clients' name, so the distributor couldn't go behind my back and cut a deal direct with them – not that I didn't trust him – but why tempt the fates? He said that would be virtually impossible because there were only three prototype projectors and all three were committed elsewhere on the date I was requesting.

I pushed and begged and he said the best he could do would be to fly one demo unit from a meeting in LA directly to the one in Hawaii. A courier would have to rush it from the airport straight to whoever was waiting for it. Well, if that was all we could do, then that was what we would do. I was glad to pay whatever for the courier or whatever extra charges would be incurred in getting the projector to my client on time. But the solution made me a bit uncomfortable, because it required telling the distributor which meeting the demo model was to be delivered to. Also, there was something not wholly kosher about this distributor. He talked too fast, even for New York, and rarely looked you in the eye. And when he did, you wished he hadn't. There was an uncomfortable tinge of the scrappy ethnic immigrant fighting ferociously for an edge, the flash in the eye of bargainers' blood-lust, the utterly craven "binessman" in its highest, or lowest if you prefer, form.

But then, why was I worried? I had in my tight, young mitts the sacrosanct, all-powerful ITT Purchase Order. Ha, take that! A bona fide PO, executed by an empowered officer of the corporation. I had, in turn, ordered 100 Fairchilds and 30 Bohn Bentons, and included my company check for the appropriate down payment for the goods, and the distributor had promised me to deliver them by the date indicated in my PO. Nothing could possibly go wrong now – all the balls were in the air – it was fait accompli.

This transaction put to bed, I was scheduled for a long-overdue honeymoon. My wife and I were going to Garmisch-Partenkirchen, a ski area in the Alps. We were going to enjoy some of our fabulous anticipated earnings as merchants and bourgeois businesspeople.

So, without further ado, I gave my distributor the name of the executive at ITT, and the hotel in Hawaii where he would be waiting for the demo unit. And my wife and I got on a plane for Germany.

Garmisch-Partenkirchen is a stunning work of Mother Nature. It's a pretty well-kept secret; few American tourists have it at the top of their wish list, and jet-setters don't consider it chic enough to be on their agenda. But the Alps that surround the town are breathtaking, and the skiing is spectacular. The twin towns are charming and Alpine to the hilt.

My wife and I checked into a handsome, quiet inn at the foot of a mountain that filled our windows, and required a craned neck to see the mountain tops disappear in the calendar-perfect cotton-puff clouds above. We were enjoying our first Continental breakfast when the landlady told me I had a long-distance call from New York. I got up, followed her into her office, and took the call. When I returned to the table my emotional state must have been apparent on the blanched rictus that had, only moments ago, been my face.

"What?" my wife asked.

"We've just been, uh, shafted," I said, slumping into my chair. "That was Norman, my client from ITT. He just canceled the purchase order for the projectors."

"Oh, my God. But...you're kidding."

"He said he just learned that he wasn't authorized to place such a large order without running it by Purchasing, who told him they had just gotten a better deal from my distributor, and they had to go with it."

"Wha... Ulch... Scrumflhh," my wife sputtered, bread crumbs falling from her flabbergasted and rapidly numbing lower lip. "But... how?" she cried at last.

"I had to tell my distributor my client's name, and that it was the ITT WorldCom meeting, so his courier could deliver the demo projector to him in Hawaii. Five seconds later evidently my distributor called ITT."

"But, he can't *do* that! It's unethical, and... And it's illegal," fumed my wife, who knew about business, and had actual wretched merchants in her gene pool.

"Well, he did it anyway."

"But, but, we have a PO!" she exclaimed.

"Right. Norman asked me to burn that, or it would be very uncomfortable for him. He said he'd make it up to me in future business. If I want any more projects from him, I have to 86 the PO and cancel the order. Like it never existed."

"But, it's just not fair!"

"I agree," I said, looking around at the handsome décor around us, and wishing we hadn't checked into such an exclusive place.

"Well, at least you get the $4,500 from the Bohn-Bentons," offered my wife.

"Nope. That's gone, too. The distributor handles Bohn-Benton as well. I can't possibly underbid him because as a distributor he gets stuff for below wholesale."

"Doesn't he know you'll never order from him again?"

"You think he cares? I'm sure he's already factored that in, and figured it's smarter to screw me now than wait for me to become a big customer later, which would make me harder to screw. He's a leading New York distributor... and I'm just a new kid on the block. Someone else will come along tomorrow. He doesn't need me. And he knows I won't sue, because I don't want to alienate Norman at ITT."

Postscript: I never got another piece of work from Norman Brust, ITT WorldCom, or from any of the executives I met there.

CHAPTER 2 THE DREAM OF HOME OWNERSHIP

W hen I was 13 my family and I lived in southern California. We had a house in the San Fernando Valley, and one overlooking Zuma beach, abutting Malibu. We had moved from NYC to Hollywood in 1947 so my dad could star in a movie called "It's a Joke, Son". It was a star vehicle, the first picture produced by the Eagle-Lion company, which became Paramount after making two pictures. "It's a Joke, Son" didn't do well for a number of reasons, and my dad, Kenny Delmar, was no longer a hot property in LA LA land.

Since I was 13, my parent's separation didn't really impact my lifestyle, in fact, it probably enhanced it. My mother lived in the house in the Valley, and my dad lived in the house in Zuma, which he moved into even as they were still building it.

The builders had just finished the core of the structure, which included a large family room, kitchen, master suite with a sunny bathroom, and a second bedroom. They hadn't even started on the second wing of additional bedrooms and bathrooms, and Boom, my dad moved in.

During the week I lived in the Valley with my mother, and attended school. I stayed in the Zuma house with my Dad on weekends, which was fine with me, because he was VERY laid back and non-judgmental. More a crazy old pal than a parent. I had my first surf-board and could walk to Zuma beach, I had use of a jalopy with a rumble seat and no license plate, which I could drive around Zuma canyon on the dirt roads; I had my first serious girl-friend, Veronica, who had a great smile, freckles, early bumps in her blouse, and lush pre-Raphaelite hair that Leonardo would have loved to paint. I had a very cool dog, Perro, an Australian Shepherd who just appeared one day, was nearly feral and who patrolled our 7 acres when he was around. I had a big white horse named Betsy, who someone gave to my dad, but he didn't ride her unless he was drunk, and then he kept falling off, so he gave her to me. There was no saddle, so I rode her bareback. My dad's Zuma house was an absolute heaven for a 13-year-old boy in 1954.

It nearly killed me when my parents announced to me and my kid brother that they were going to try to patch up the marriage and move back to our house at 42 East 75th Street in Manhattan, where I had mostly grown up. To be 13 in Manhattan is not heaven. There's no beach, no surfing, no un-licensed jalopy to drive, no horse to ride, no dog, except my mother's miserable miniature lap-dog, which hid under the bed, crapped and peed on everything, and bit people who tried to pet it. You couldn't walk around in a bathing suit and flip-flops. And you couldn't even ride a bicycle -- it was too dangerous. The only fun thing to do for a boy in Manhattan was to sneak into Central Park and pretend you were in the country. Although you couldn't even climb a tree because some cop would yell at you to get down. You couldn't throw an acorn to a squirrel because some tree-hugger would bring you up on charges of animal cruelty.

The only silver lining about living in the Big Apple was that in the eighth grade at PS-6, I fell hopelessly in love with Lynn Rushmore. I was class president and she was the secretary. I gave her a gold locket, and occasionally followed her when she walked home, my heart pounding. She was the sweetest, coolest, most angelic-looking girl I had ever seen. Her voice was a mixture of honey and caramel. Everyone was in love with her, boys, girls, teachers, animals. I got to kiss her once, Oh my God, at a spin-the-bottle party. And I danced with her once, to "Mr. Sandman," a slow one. She was in my arms and her cheek touched mine a few times. I forgot to breathe and nearly passed out. But I was too shy and too young. When I asked her to the school dance, she was already going with someone else, a bug-eyed guy who talked too loud and wore a gauche white tuxedo. No, really. He looked like he just stepped out of a Good Humor truck.

Then Lynn and I graduated. My parents sent me to the ultra-exclusive Trinity School, and Lynn went off to the High School of Music and Art. We drifted apart, but I was always anxious to get any news about her and what she was doing.

Then, in 1958, our junior year in high school, Lynn's father, Howard Rushmore, who was having financial problems and had become mentally unstable, shot Lynn's mother and himself to death in a NY Taxicab. It was all over the news. I went to the Frank E. Campbell Funeral Chapel on Madison Avenue to attend the funeral and throw myself at Lynn's feet and declare my undying love, or hold her in my arms while she wept, or just get a glimpse of her, but the goons at the door wouldn't let me in because I was just some kid, and my name wasn't on the guest list. Lynn vanished, changed her name and moved away and I never heard or saw anything about her again. Today, 60 years later, I think about her at least once a day and wonder what happened to her and if she is okay. (I recently learned that she met and married some guy who went to Princeton, and is currently living in a 6,000 square foot house in Miami. I was very relieved to learn that she found a happy ending.)

About this time, my dad was wondering why the UCLA professor with four kids who was renting his Zuma house had stopped sending the rent. Dad called the professor and asked what the problem was, and the professor explained that the California Marshall had told him that Kenny Delmar had not paid his taxes for six years, and now the property was owned by the County of Los Angeles. My dad booked a flight to LA the next day.

Dad rented a car at LAX and drove to the US Marshals Service office in Los Angeles. He asked them what was going on with his property in Zuma. The Deputy looked it up and said, "I'm sorry, Mr. Delmar, but you neglected to pay your real estate taxes on that parcel for five years, plus the year during which you can maybe plead with the county to rescind the sale, and the parcel was acquired by the tax collector and turned over to the County of Los Angeles."

Dad spent the rest of the week driving around to various City offices and bureaus, pleading with officials and talking to attorneys.

If you don't pay your property taxes in California, the delinquent amount (which includes taxes, interest, penalties, and costs resulting from the delinquency) becomes a lien on your home, and the tax collector can, and usually does, sell the place in a public auction.

In California, the tax collector must send you a written notice by certified mail not less than 45 days nor more than 120 days before the sale, as well as try his best to contact you, if possible, before selling your home in a tax sale. The tax man only had three addresses for Kenny Delmar, the house in Zuma, the long-ago-sold house in San Fernando Valley, and 42 East 75th Street in Manhattan. No mail sent to those addresses was ever answered. The phone lines to the Zuma house and the Valley house had both been shut down. And there was no way to contact my Dad, who was living some 3,000 miles away, and not in the house he was supposed to be living in. The tax man is also obliged to publish the notice in the local newspaper, which he did, but no one in the Delmar family was reading the "Los Angeles Tribune" in 1959.

The only way to stop the tax sale and redeem the house is by paying the delinquent taxes. You have a right to set up a payment plan with the tax collector. So long as you keep up on the installments, the collector cannot proceed with a sale.

At the auction of your house, the winning bid must be at least the amount of the unpaid taxes plus, penalties, costs and a redemption fee.

In California, you don't get the right to redeem the home after the sale. However, if your home doesn't sell at the auction or the purchaser who bought it at the sale backs out of the deal, or does not perform, your right to redeem revives. This means you can still pay off the debt to save your home if the buyer fails to perform per the rules of the auction.

However, the Delmar property on Zuma was not sold to a buyer at auction, but turned over to the County of Los Angeles by the tax collector, at his discretion.

One attorney told my dad that he might be able to get his home back by filing a petition within one year convincing the Board of Supervisors of the County of Los Angeles to rescind the sale or transfer. He would have to show that the sale or transfer was invalid for some legal reason, or prove the procedures were not proper. Dad's attorney warned him that the petitioner almost NEVER won.

Dad contacted the legal department of Screen Actors Guild in LA, and also called his friend, Frank Sinatra, to intercede, as Sinatra was a buddy of Sam Yorty, Mayor of LA at the time, and also a pal of Pat Brown, the then governor of California. Hearing about the coming legal actions from SAG, and recognizing the pressure that would come from Yorty and Brown, The County of Los Angeles quickly sold this prime piece of Zuma property to the State of California for one dollar. The state promptly declared it "parkland." Brown, Yorty, SAG and Sinatra reported to my father that he would have to fuggedaboudit. His Zuma home was gone, gone, gone, forever and ever, period.

* * *

Last time I was in LA, about fifteen years ago, I drove out to Trancas Canyon Road, a right turn off the PCH, (Pacific Coast Highway), that wound its way up Zuma Canyon to where Dad's 7.5 acres and California ranch house used to be. Dad's old house site was not accessible as the road ended in an imposing gate that kept the hoi polloi away from the stunning community of Wow McMansions beyond. I could see where dad's house used to be, but it was gone, now replaced by an imposing California mansion.

Dad bought the choice piece of land from Irwin Shaw, in 1953 or '54, for, I believe, a thousand an acre, or $7,500. The real estate taxes were a mere $135 per year! The bills and certified mail from the tax collector warning of the impending tax sale had been arriving for years at 42 East 75th Street, where my Mother Dearest had been vindictively throwing them in the trash.

She did this because when she was in the hospital giving birth to my kid brother in 1948, one of her closest lady friends informed her that my father was having an affair with this Tennessee woman, Barbara, and had been seeing her for years. This was back in the day when plenty of wives were stifling such information, and turning a blind eye, especially if their husbands were doing really well. The Barbara thing was not a passing fancy. She was in my father's life for decades, on and off. And in fact, when he moved into the house in Zuma, she followed soon after, having driven all the way across the country in two and a half days, more or less non-stop.

When I went to stay with my dad out at the ranch as usual one Friday evening, Barbara was there, and my dad introduced her to me as his housekeeper. Parents are so cute, don't they know that 13-year-olds know *everything*? So I suppose it's no wonder that my mother, Alice, was throwing the tax bills for Zuma in the trash, although it seems in retrospect a colossally stupid thing to do, like cutting off your nose to spite your face, as she was destined to inherit everything he left, and if he had received the warnings, paid the picayune taxes and kept the property, she would have inherited millions from the Zuma property. Well, she sure taught him a lesson.

CHAPTER 3   FRIENDS WILL HELP YOU GET A JOB

My father, the late Kenny Delmar, was an actor and radio personality. A close, old friend of his, Wayne Howell, (real name Wayne Chapelle) had been an announcer and voice-over man for NBC for years, and told us that he had a strong hand in hiring and firing of on-camera news reporters at NBC in Manhattan. My dad and I were having a couple of drinks with Wayne at his plush Manhattan apartment on west 47th Street, above the diamond district one evening in the mid 70's when suddenly Wayne asked me, "So, Ken, what are you making annually as a filmmaker?" "It varies," I said. I'm at about a hundred a year right now."

"How would you like to triple that as an NBC newscaster?" said Wayne. "And that's just for starters. You'd be making over a million a year within three, four years."

"Uh...Jeez," I said.

"Nothing to it," said Wayne. "Can you read a prompter?"

"Sure, I can read a prompter," I said.

"Okay, I'm gonna set you up an audition," said Wayne. "But don't worry, it's just a formality, because I'm the guy who judges the audition." He set up an audition for me for a week later.

To prepare, I set up a video camera, three movie lights and a TelePrompTer (this was easy, as I was already in the film/video business and had all these things). I got my production assistant to operate the camera, and my admin to operate the TelePrompter, and rehearsed my butt off every day that week.

I went to the audition Wayne set up and read the copy on the prompter and ad-libbed when the prompter suddenly went dead (I had been warned that this was part of the audition). It went very well and I was happy with my performance. After the audition Wayne took me and my father to his apartment for drinks and a debriefing.

"Your audition was terrific," Wayne said after a sip of his 25 year-old single-malt scotch on the rocks. "One of the best I've seen."

"But...?" I said.

"But, nothing," he said. "I'm ready to hire you and start you on your way. I'll get behind you and promote you and put you on the fast track. In three years you'll be a hot property, and a millionaire. There's only one thing: I get fifty percent of your net income for the duration of your broadcasting career. And that's cash, Slick. I can't have Uncle Sam thinking I'm making more than I do."

"Fifty percent!" my father gasped. "Th... that's almost half!" Always the comedian.

"Right. But so what?" said Wayne to me. "You'll be making a million a year, just for starters. That's a half a million dollars for you, just for combing your hair, putting on a jacket and tie, and reading copy off a prompter every morning. *Reading*, babe. You don't have to write, you don't have to chase down stories, and you don't even have to think. In fact, it's better if you *don't* think. A half million a year is a lot more than you're making now working your ass off as a free-lance videographer. What do you care what I do with my half?"

"I... I... I..." I muttered, looking at my father, who was trying hard not to look flabbergasted himself.

"Jesus, Wayne," dad said, "Fifty percent?"

"Yes, dad," I said. "Ha... hann... hrgg... *half*." It had just never occurred to naïve, doe-eyed me that somebody would offer someone a job, and then demand *half* their income for the rest of their professional life! And here was this man, purportedly a friend of my father's, sitting there with a straight face, glib air, and single malt scotch as if he were making a perfectly reasonable proposal.

"Holy shit" I muttered.

"That's right," said Wayne.

"And you want your half in cash?" I mumbled, still lost in flabbergastedness.

"Take it or leave it," said Wayne.

"How about a third?" I offered. "I think I could maybe live with 33 percent."

"Nah, fifty," said Wayne. "I'm giving you this break, Kenny, because your dad and I have known each other for so long." My dad was still trying to get control of his face, although one of his eyes had surrendered to an uncontrollable nervous tic.

"Well," I said, "I'd like to think about it."

"Sure," said Wayne. "Take a minute."

"I mean, go home and sleep on it. Discuss it with my wife."

"Forget it," said Wayne. "Fuck your wife. It's simple: Do you want to become a TV anchorman and live the life of Riley, or do you want to slave away like an ignorant laborer, shooting low-budget industrials and crappy test commercials for the rest of your life?"

"Well, you know what," I said, "I guess I'll pass. Fuck Riley." My dudgeon had risen suddenly, I don't know why.

"Okay, then," said Wayne with a shrug, "your call." He wasn't angry or bitter, this was just a bit of business taken care of. I had proven to be some sort of puritanical, simple-minded rube who couldn't imagine giving some self-important penis *half* his earnings, in cash, tax free, for the rest of his working life.

Later, riding with my father in his car back to Connecticut, he was lost in thought and had nothing to say for a long while, which was rare.

"So, are you angry with me?" I asked.

"No. I was just thinking, we blew it. You should have taken the job, and then in a year or so we coulda had him killed. Yaya

26

knows a guy in the mafia. He could have made it look like an accident."

"Damn. Why didn't I think of that?"

"Bad upbringing."

* * *

Wayne Howell died in 1986 at age 72. So if I had taken his deal in '76, it would have only been ten years of paying him half my earning in cash under the table, if I didn't have him killed like my dad half-humorously suggested. Figuring the anticipated income of roughly $350,000 a year the first year, and then rising to a million a year by year four, assuming I did well and was appropriately promoted, I would have paid Wayne around $3.8 million. And I would have made $3.8 million. Hmm. That's a lot more than I made with my film production company. And that was a lot of work. Plus plenty of stress. I felt responsible to keep business coming in so I would be able to pay my staff. They depended on me. That was an alabatross around my neck.

As a newscaster, I would have only been required to show up with a decent voice, a pleasant face, a civilized haircut, and an ability to read aloud from a prompter. Plus only work for a couple of hours a day. So, in retrospect, did I make the right decision in telling Wayne to stick it where the sun don't shine? Interestingly, if he had agreed to take only a third instead of half, I would have done it. By being greedy, Wayne lost a passive income of millions. I hope that was a good lesson for him. Listen to this – I'm such a naif. Don't I understand that I was replaced within hours, if not minutes, by some other young guy who could read a prompter and speak clearly? I hope that whoever it was had the sense to hire someone to take care of Wayne, and everyone like him, and make it look like an accident. And yes, I'm suggesting this half-humorously

CHAPTER 4   PAY TO PLAY

When I was operating my film & video production company in NYC, a friend of an associate referred me to a potential new piece of business. A major horse-racing organization wanted a film made, a corporate image piece, and money was no object. The contact was not the decision-maker at the company, a man in his sixties, but the woman who was sleeping with him. Let's call her Miss Scarlet. This woman, in her mid-forties but well-preserved and still attractive, wasn't just his pillow partner; she was a southern lady with the full-on southern accent, the haughty look, designer clothes and tasteful jewelry. She had actually worked, once upon a time, for a broadcast marketing firm, although she didn't talk about that because proper ladies don't work.

I called her and she said that she wanted to meet me at her Manhattan apartment rather than see me at my offices. I could hear the pages of her Southern Belle Manipulation Manual flipping in the background. I mentioned I wanted to bring one of my producers to the meeting. Not acceptable. Fine. Whatever.

I went to her apartment alone. I had nothing to lose; if I didn't want to dance her dance, I could say no and walk out, nothing lost.

Her apartment was in a nice East-side neighborhood. The doorman called up, then gave me her floor, and apartment number, and directed me to the elevators.

Miss Scarlet opened her door herself, since the damned Yankees, in their thoughtless and brutish War of Northern Aggression, had destroyed everything genteel and cultured, and had made it virtually impossible for any decent person of breeding who was not a billionaire, or married to one, to have full time domestic help.

Miss Scarlet was trim and handsome, haughty in the manner of up-scale southern folk, well-groomed and well-dressed. She introduced herself, shook my hand firmly, and ushered me into her fastidiously maintained living room. She was polite, but not at all overly hospitable and gushy the way Yankees expect southern women to be. More the tough businesswoman – the iron hand in the velvet glove. I heard the theme from "Steel Magnolias" playing in the background.

I was invited to sit in a carved rosewood Victorian sofa. Miss Scarlet sat across from me in an ante-bellum wing-chair with threadbare silk upholstery hanging on by a hair of its chinny-chin-chin. For one wild nanosecond I found myself checking to see if her dress was made from the same fabric as the drapes.

The apartment was sparely decorated with a few handsome antiques. Miss Scarlet asked me if I would like a lemonade, iced tea, or a glass of sherry. I opted for the iced tea. The sherry would have been a bad choice, as anything that slowed me down or dulled my senses would have been a mistake.

The iced tea was delivered by Miss Scarlet's daughter, a pretty, dark-eyed girl of around seventeen, who was introduced, shook my hand, curtseyed, smiled pleasantly, and left the apartment immediately. I got the feeling that my hostess was displeased to have such an old daughter, who by her advanced age compromised the effect of Miss Scarlet's almost imperceptible face-lift.

Miss Scarlet got right into the meat of what sort of film she envisioned. I nodded and listened closely. It was made very clear that the awarding of the contract was very much in her control. I asked her if she would like to see some of our action work, or a couple of our corporate image pieces, but she said that wasn't necessary. She had already checked me out through her sources, and had ascertained that we were more than qualified to do the job. She didn't beat around the bush, but came right out with the key parameters of the job: the objective, the target audience, the deadline, and the budget.

"Sixty percent of the gross is mine," she said finally. She stopped talking and looked at me with a flinty blinkless stare.

"What?" I said, as I felt my chin separate from my skull and come to rest on my neatly knotted tie.

"You heard me, darlin'" she said. "I said sixty percent of the gross is mine. Off the top."

"Hahnrg," I said, having lost control of my ability to speak. "Humph, flulgll, woiks... Excuse me. But I think I misunderstood you, ha ha. I thought you just said *sixty percent of the gross.*"

"You understood me perfectly, honey. I give you the job, and you give me sixty percent of the gross. In cash. I want you to bill the company in thirds, and I want you to pay me three payments, in cash, within three business days of when you receive your checks for each third. Is there any of that you don't understand?"

A joke, right? I thought. Candid Camera behind the curtain? But I said, "Uhhhh."

"So, darlin'" she said evenly, "Are you in or not?"

"Um, just a thought – how am I supposed to produce the film if I give you sixty percent of the budget?"

"Oh, come on, Delmar. I've worked in production. I know you can do a lovely job with the remaining forty percent, and make a profit in the process. Plus, I only want one third of the print and video dub budget, so you'll be able to make it up there."

"Okay, I'll be leaving now," I said rising. Miss Scarlet could detect from my tone and body language that I was serious about walking out.

"Why, Kenny Delmar, I thought you were a businessman. Don't you even intend to make a counteroffer?"

"Counteroffer? I'm not trying to buy your house, Miss Scarlet. I'm just a humble producer trying to earn enough money to make payroll and keep my kid in shoes."

"Okay, if you insist. I'll come down to fifty percent."

"Good-bye." I offered my hand.

"Forty five, but that's my final offer."

"It's been a pleasure," I said. And since Miss Scarlet hadn't bothered to rise, or shake my hand, I turned to let myself out.

"You're a ruthless son of a bitch Yankee horse-trader," Miss Scarlet said evenly through her teeth. "What the hell do you want?"

"I'll pay a standard finder's fee of ten percent, and that's it."

"Oh, darlin', you're so full of shit."

"I'm sorry. That's all I can offer you, and be sure I can do a good job, plus cover my overhead."

"Blah, blah, blah. Then I want one hundred percent of the profit."

"Miss Scarlet, no disrespect intended, but no one on the face of this earth is going to pay you one hundred percent of anything."

"Well, you're wrong about that, young man. I have steered several pieces of business here and there in this city and on both sides of the Mason Dixon Line for one hundred percent of the profit. And those who got the jobs are tickled pink to be working with me."

"Well, that's lovely. But I'm in business to make a profit, so thank you very much, and good afternoon." I turned and exited the apartment. I was in the vestibule waiting for the elevator when Miss Scarlet opened her door.

"All right, you win," she purred. "I'll settle for seventy five percent of the profit. But I want access to the books, and I want detailed accounting. And I mean the *real* books." I considered her proposal. The film was an interesting project, with color and action and outdoor shooting in the summer, and creative would be left to me. We had nothing else engaging to do that summer. I thought the job would be fun, and I knew my staff would enjoy doing it. I approached Miss Scarlet and offered her my hand.

"I can split the profit with you," I said. "Fifty-fifty, but that's it."

"Oh, you're killing me," she said. "How will I be able to pay my daughter's tuition at Spence? You're taking the food right out of our mouths, you damn Yankee monster. Okay, it's a deal."

"Deal," I said, shaking her hand.

"Oh, good," she purred. "You're such a lovely man. We're going to have an absolutely delightful time with this film. I just know you're going to do a wonderful job, and we're all going to love it." She drew me back into her foyer, hugged me and kissed me on the cheek. "You're such a brute of a horse-trader."

"Well, I'm sure it's going to be great fun."

"Now, you understand that I have to be paid in fifties and hundreds, and not brand new ones, of course."

"Confederate isn't good?" I quipped, and we laughed together.

"Off the books. And don't be asking me to sign anything, Sugar."

"Uh huh."

"I want that delivered by you in person and alone, to me in person, to a place I designate. And don't try to play me out, or fuck me around, darlin', because I'll know to the minute when the Racing Association checks go out the door."

"Okay, no problem," I said.

This production actually did turn out to be fun, because when I did it we had a big budget and I went first class. When the picture was delivered and accepted, it was gorgeous and wonderful, but alas, there was only $1,290.00 profit. I dutifully gave Miss Scarlet her 50%, which was $645.00, along with a detailed copy of the production books, with every penny accounted for. I can remember the expression on her face to this day. The amazing thing is that she didn't pull a pearl-handled Derringer from beneath her petticoats and shoot my wretched Yankee ass right then and there.

Needless to say, she didn't steer any future business our way, and that just broke our damn Yankee hearts.

CHAPTER 5   THEY CAN'T KEEP A GOOD PERSON DOWN

I have changed the names of the principal players in this tale, as some of them are still alive, and some of them are rich and powerful enough to hire lawyers and sue me, and I just don't have the time for that. Also, I have a new car and I would be very unhappy if it and I were crushed by a cement truck at a crossing (read on). This is, in places, a quasi-dramatized telling of the events. The quotations, for example, are my best efforts to recreate the gist of the scene, and not meant to be verbatim.

On several occasions I have had to bridge the blanks, or tell portions of the story with information gleaned from one side or the other, or from third parties. But the lion's share of what I recount below is taken from scenes I was in, or information that came directly to me from the principal player, (name altered) Sherry Lund. With these disclaimers, I want you to know that I have done my best to present the true story.

I was sitting in my production company office in New York's Time & Life building one afternoon, trying to look like I was thinking important thoughts to reassure my underpaid staff, when a slender, white-haired, smartly-dressed woman in her seventies, and a girl of perhaps fifteen swept past my receptionist and burst into my office unannounced. Before I could say "What the..." the older woman plunked a bottle of Hennessey Special Reserve Cognac down on my desk.

The woman had already got my attention, however, with her young companion, who was a show-stopper, with stunning boudoir eyes, kiss-me-please lips, spread-me-on-a-pillow hair, and a gushing bodice begging to be ripped asunder by a passing random heterosexual pirate. The girl was lush and dark; Mediterranean-looking, like maybe Italian or Jewish, with dark brown hair and eyes, light mocha skin. Her body language suggested she was torn between embarrassment and mortification. The older woman promptly took a seat at the foot of my desk, and directed her stunning young ward to another. The girl rolled her eyes, apologizing to me for her guardian's aggressiveness. I gestured for the girl to please take a seat. She did, crossed her legs, and her skirt rode up her thigh. She pulled the hem back down. The older woman reached over and pushed it back up, and then some.

"Don't ever be ashamed of what you've got, honey," said the woman. The girl rolled her eyes again, blushing to the roots, and looked at me for sympathy.

"Kenny," said the woman, like she had known me for decades, "this is my granddaughter, (or maybe she said God-daughter) Sherry Lund. She's come to The Big Apple to get her start in music. She sings, Kenny, and what a voice. She knows how to sell a song. She's a natural, Kenny. Sings like Lady Day, writes lyrics like Lennon and music like Gershwin. Not only that, she can act.

"*Grammy!*" objected the young lady, batting lush eyelashes that could have swept my office clean with three strokes.

"Kenny," the woman continued, "I want you to represent my beautiful and talented Sherry. You're the only one I trust. Look at her. Is she easy to look at, or what?"

I looked at her. She certainly was easy to look at. "How old are you?" I asked.

"Fourteen," said the young lady, just as Granny said, "Seventeen."

"Whatever," Granny continued. "She's got a wide range. She can play thirteen, she can play twenty five. Put makeup and a wig on her, she can play Methuselah. Can you handle her, Kenny? Oh my God, you gotta hear her sing?"

"Umm," I said. Always witty.

"Sing, honey," Granny cued her ward. "Sing!" Sherry took a breath, and all of a sudden the room was filled with this astounding voice. This divine young beauty, who I was ready to buy on looks alone, had the pipes of an Ethel Merman, the soul of Billie Holliday, the clarity of Whitney Houston, and the range of Mariah Carey. I closed my eyes and the voice conjured up a black woman of thirty five or so, a 180 pound pumpernickel Mother Earth with all the pathos, passion, love, and suffering of the world shot through the fiber of her long-suffering soul. She was singing, a capella, in perfect pitch, a pop love song -- and knocking my Argyle socks off.

"Stop," I said, holding up my hand. "Sherry, you're huge, kickass, a natural, but I can't represent you, because I'm not an agent. But don't worry – my friend up the hall is. I'll send you to him and he'll represent you. And if he says no, I'll send you to another friend at William Morris."

"Oh, Kenny, you're such a sweetheart," said Grammy, rising, shaking my hand and pulling me into a hug. "I knew I could rely on you. Thank you. Thank you a thousand times. Who's the agent up the hall?"

"Archer King."

"Oh, I've heard of him," said Grammy. "Can you call him now? We're here, so maybe he could see us now, if it wouldn't be an imposition. What do you think?"

I picked up the phone and dialed Archer. He was in, and, upon my rave recommendation, agreed to see Sherry.

"Take your bottle of cognac" I said to Grammy as I showed her and her young charge to the door.

"No, honey," she said. "That's yours. I only wish it were a case. You gave Sherry her first break, sweetheart. Enjoy, and God bless."

Archer called me later and agreed Sherry was gifted and gorgeous and had real potential. He said he would do what he could for her, but that he was concerned about the grandmother, or godmother, or whatever the hell she was, getting in the way. Archer passed Sherry on to another agent, someone who specialized in musicians and vocalists.

Young Sherry's singing career didn't explode like some superstar discoveree from Schwab's Drugstore in Hollywood – she was too young -- but she hung in while finishing high school, and worked in her field, and honed her craft with tenacity and devotion.

Over the next couple of years I got occasional cards, calls and drop-ins from Sherry, who knew it was smart to stay in touch, and who I liked, so I was glad to have her do so. I didn't have any work for her, as I sub-contracted out for any music I might use for my productions. I would have used her for on-camera or voice-over work if she was right for something, but she wasn't in the appropriate unions yet, and I was a signatory to those SAG and AFTRA contracts as a producer.

Sherry was finishing high school in her spare time, the way talent does in the city, while chipping away at trying to get her break. She was writing songs, and auditioning for jingles, and singing when and where she could. At seventeen, she moved into Manhattan with two other young female aspirants, into a decent apartment building on the East side that they could just barely afford by eliminating food and clothing, but it was worth it because it was a good neighborhood, and there was a 24/7 doorman.

They gave a cocktail party every once in a while for people they were meeting in the city, and networked like mad. I attended a couple of those parties, and they were very well done, with delicious homemade canapés and everyone polite and earnest and good-looking and upwardly mobile. New York show-business and advertising yuppies rubbed elbows with their peers and people who could give them work, or already had. As I recall, I was surprised that I didn't see anyone snorting lines of cocaine off the coffee table. They were, for Manhattan at the time, surprisingly straight affairs.

All three of the young women had part-time jobs to support them while they showcased and auditioned and trained and did what they could to get their break.

One of the girls got a small running part in a TV sitcom, and immediately moved out to the coast. Covering the shortfall was scary for a while for Sherry and her remaining roommate. Soon, Sherry was running herself ragged, with various part-time jobs, and the auditions and training and trying to find a group to sing with, etc. To keep up, my guess is she probably started using some sort of uppers at this point, diet pills, or maybe some coke given to her by a well-fixed boyfriend, like virtually every other young actor, male or female, in New York City, but I'm just surmising.

On the social front, I counseled her not to waste her time on handsome bad-boy goons, but to try to date the right men, men that might be in a position to help her career. I became her Dutch uncle, or father-figure, and she would come by the office occasionally and we would talk. I would give my Yoda-like advice, she would chatter on about this and that experience. I enjoyed the relationship, and felt it kept me connected with an age bracket and a milieu of New York that I had grown unfamiliar with.

You couldn't help liking Sherry. She was the proverbial ray of sunshine, a breath of fresh air. She was the earnest shiny-faced ingénue in the ongoing musical comedy of the Big Apple; so full of unalloyed high hopes, you couldn't help but get caught up in her youthful enthusiasm and great expectations. You wanted to help, to do what you could to help her make her dream come true. And also, she was so gifted, you just knew that she would make it. You knew that eventually, one way or another, irresistibly, her star would ascend.

Sherry moved out to southern California, and we lost touch for a while. I heard from mutual friends that she had fallen in with the head of a successful motion picture lighting equipment company, and he had financed her move to Marina del Rey, and they were living together there in a condo on the water. She was writing songs, and putting a small band together, doing some gigs, and looking for representation. That was the last I heard of or about Sherry for a couple of years, until she called one day in 1977 and said she was in New York to take dubs of her demo tape around to all the key New York music houses, hoping to get jingle work. She asked if she could come by and have my sound guy make a few audio dubs of her master tape. Sure, I said, my pleasure.

Sherry's tape was a quarter inch reel-to-reel duplicate master of two tunes performed by her and a small rock group she had put together. The musicians were four California guys; keyboard, guitar, bass, and drums. They weren't the Beatles, but they made decent music together.

Commercial TV and radio jingle work supports more musicians in New York than any other single activity except maybe unemployment insurance. If the spots are for big name clients, and run on National TV for a half a year or more, the residuals for the composer, singers and soloists can make their year. Background studio musicians make less, but jingle gigs grease the ways, and make it possible to conduct an ongoing career in music, while waiting for one's big break.

Sherry had called Smashing Music (fabricated name), one of New York's major jingle houses and asked if she could drop by, introduce herself and leave an audio dub. They said okay.

"I'd like to hear it," I said to Sherry. "Do you mind if my engineer feeds it in here while he's making the dubs?"

"No, please, I want your opinion."

Tim, my audio engineer, sent the audio signal to the speakers in my office, and Sherry and I sat there and listened to her performance of "Better Be Real." (Not the real name of the tune.) It was a long cut, nearly four minutes, but you were sorry when it ended, because it was clearly a kickass hit. Sherry was the only vocalist; she had dubbed over herself for a few choruses, but it was her doing all the singing.

"Wow," I said, when the tune rang off. "That was *huge!*"

"Right. Now tell me what you really think."

"I think it's ready to go on the air and win the Grammies."

"Oh, c'mon."

"I'm dead serious. It's a kickass tune, and you know it. Who wrote the lyrics?"

"Me."

"And the music?"

"Me."

"Sherry, you're a genius, a gorgeous, young genius with a kickass hit on your hands!"

"You're making me blush."

"I mean it. You could go straight to air with it. Make it the hit single leader for an album."

"Well, thank you. Let's just hope that some of the jingle houses like it as much as you do."

"I wish I knew someone at one of the big record companies. With a tune like that, and your voice, they'd sign you in a second."

"Well, thanks, but I'm willing to crawl before I walk."

"You must know someone at a label. Or know someone who knows someone at a label?"

"No. That's why I'm schlepping my demo around."

My audio engineer made Sherry a dozen cassettes, and we made up labels and affixed them for her, no charge. I wished her luck, and sent her on her way. I told her I had an out of town shoot for a several days, so not to bother following up with me until she got back to the coast. So she bid me adieu, thanked us, and went out to distribute her demos.

When I got back from my out-of-town shoot, Tim told me that Sherry had come back the following afternoon and asked him to make a quarter-inch reel-to-reel dub of her master. Seems someone at Smashing Music had gotten it wrong: they *did* want a quarter-inch reel-to-reel of her demo instead of the usual cassette.

Hmmm, that didn't sound right. Why would they want a quarter-inch dub of the master? An audio cassette dub is standard for a demo, and has plenty of quality for a demo listen. A quarter-inch reel-to-reel is what you would use to reproduce the music on other media. The hairs went up on the back on my neck. Tim and I looked at one another thinking the same thing. After a beat, he shrugged, and I shrugged back.

Three months later, in the winter of 1978 I was on vacation with my wife, climbing into a double-chair ski-lift in Keystone, Colorado, when I heard a familiar tune on the portable radio the lift attendant had hung from the stanchion behind her. It was "Better Be Real," (not the real title) by Sherry Lund, and the announcer had just said that it had hit number eight of the top ten, and was climbing the charts fast.

"Oh, wow!" I said to my wife. "Sherry's on her way," I said. "I can't believe it, how fast it happened. Just amazing."

We heard the tune several more times, in Colorado, and when we returned to Connecticut, as it climbed the charts to number one. To congratulate her, and get the inside story, I tried a couple of times to call Sherry's number in Marina del Rey, but only got the answering machine. Then one day a few weeks later, she called me.

"I'm in New York," she said. "With my lawyers."

"Your lawyers?"

"It's a long story. Can I come by?"

Two hours later Sherry appeared and told me why she was traveling with lawyers.

After she left my office with her audio dubs, Sherry went into the canyons of Manhattan to distribute her samples to the top jingle houses and recording studios. She was going in person because she was eminently presentable and winsome, and because an in-the-flesh appearance will always make a stronger impression than some impersonal medium (read my book, *Winning Moves, Body Language for Business*). One of the first places Sherry went was Smashing Music. She gave them a dub of the audio tape, an 8x10" head-shot with a resume on the back; standard talent stuff. The head of the office, Jimmy Lesewer, (not his real name) listened to her dub, and soon thereafter, someone from Smashing Music told Sherry that the audio dub didn't have enough fidelity for them, and to bring or send over a quarter-inch dub. This is why Sherry came back to the office and asked Tim to make her a quarter-inch duplicate of her master tape. And this is the dub that she took back to Smashing.

Sherry finished distributing her dubs and head-shots and returned to Marina del Rey. She got a couple of gigs on the coast, just enough to keep her afloat, but nothing big enough to require flying back to New York. She didn't hear anything from Smashing, or anyone else in New York, until the day she was driving along the Pacific Coast Highway and heard her tune "Better Be Real" on the radio, climbing the charts! A few phone calls later and she learned that the tune had been acquired from Smashing Music by Colossal Records (names changed to protect the guilty), and that it was being distributed by them, and that they had signed Sherry Lund, this kick-ass new black singer, who was slated to make appearances on upcoming TV shows!

"But, but, but, *I'm* Sherry Lund!" Sherry cried over the phone to the man at Colossal.

"Sure you are," said the voice on the other end, and hung up.

Sherry called Mr. Lesewer at Smashing and asked him what the hell was going on.

"Who's this?" he asked.

"I told you who this is," said Sherry, nearly choking on her rage. "Sherry Lund. I brought you a dub of "Better Be Real," a couple of months ago. You listened to my demo. Someone in your office asked for a quarter-inch reel-to-reel dub. So I brought you a quarter-inch dub. Now I hear the tune climbing the charts, and that someone else, some black singer, is about to make TV appearances posing as me, using my name!"

"Uh, Sherry, I'm sorry, but I couldn't reach you. We had no address. We had no phone number and there was none in the book. We tried SAG, We tried AFTRA, and AGVA, but you didn't exist. You had just disappeared into thin air. Colossal loved the tune, and the voice, and they wanted to sign the artist right away. What was I supposed to do?"

"Couldn't reach me? Couldn't reach me? Did you try ringing the number on the tape? My number was all over my demo. And on my head-shot."

"It may have been on the audio dub, but all that was on the quarter-inch was some hand-written thing that got smudged. We couldn't read it. We tried all the California directories, and the Player's Guide, and no one had a number for you, or knew where you were. No one ever heard of you."

"I left a head-shot and resume. That had my number on it, too."

"Oh, we throw those out half the time. We get dozens of those a day. No one could find it."

"This is such bullshit."

"I'm sorry, I can't help you. It's all over and done with."

"Colossal said they paid you one hundred thousand dollars for my single, "Better Be Real." Where is that money?!"

"That's a question for my attorney. I'm not supposed to talk to you at all. Now don't call this office, or harass me again. Good bye."

"Harass you!" howled Sherry to a dead phone. "You stole my song! You stole my music! You stole my name!"

"So, Sherry hired a lawyer, and he and his team did some digging, and met with Colossal's lawyers and here's the net of it:

Colossal had paid Lesewer of Smashing Music one hundred thousand dollars for "Better Be Real," purportedly under the impression that Lesewer represented the talent: Sherry Lund. Only five thousand dollars could be recouped from Lesewer by Sherry's lawyers, because he claimed he had used ninety-five thousand to buy his wife a new Rolls Royce Corniche. There was some horseshit legal reason why Lesewer's wife didn't have to return the car. Lesewer continued to claim he made best efforts to locate Sherry, but that she had vanished from the face of the earth.

Of course, since Sherry was living in the condo of the owner of the film truck company, it was in his name, and her number was unlisted, as most every young aspirant's number in Hollywood is unlisted. When Colossal distributed the tune, and it was a hit, they wanted to sign Sherry, and her group as well, and build an album around the hit single. Time was of the essence, because a new single by an unknown will not stay on the charts long, and if you want to capitalize on it, you have to move fast to get the album out there and build on the momentum.

Colossal had recently acquired a black singer with Sherry's sound, a woman they had picked up on after a TV talent show appearance in the mid-seventies. They gave her Sherry's name. The name "Sherry Lund" was registered with the appropriate unions, of which the real Sherry Lund was not a member, as she had not had the eight hundred dollars and change that it took at the time to join. Colossal hired writers and put together a group and forged full-steam ahead on pumping out an album. The new Sherry Lund, a black woman some fifteen years Sherry's senior, was fed into Colossal's marketing and publicity machines, gigs and appearances were booked for her, and the tune began the process of gaining momentum as the hit single of the year, with "Sherry Lund" as the brightest and best of the new talent.

So the real Sherry came to New York with her lawyers for the showdown with Colossal Records and Smashing Music. Sherry's lawyers were looking for a settlement of a couple of million dollars. It was based on what the tune, lyrics, the album and publishing rights could have, at minimum, been reasonably expected to earn for Sherry.

Here's the deal Colossal offered, told to me by the original Sherry: Whatever happened in the past was water under the bridge. Sherry's name now belonged to another woman whose handlers had joined her into SAG and AFTRA. This other woman had made appearances under Sherry's name, and recorded tunes for the album, and now had legal claims to use the name, much like a trade name. No one in entertainment used their original name anyway, so what was the big deal? The items of the music rights and copyright in the lyrics was a touchier issue. Common law and copyright law and creative property law and the tough music guilds, ASCAP and BMI are very strict and don't leave any room for skullduggery. If you create a piece of music, or write the lyrics, on our own and not as "paid for hire," those things are your property until you specifically assign them to someone else or some other corporate entity. Colossal had a proposal to handle those matters. Sherry was to sign over her music and lyrics rights in exchange for a record deal and a new name.

Meanwhile, to apply pressure, Sherry was told by her lawyers that apparently Colossal's team had hired detectives and dug into her past, and had witnesses and affidavits from men who would testify that she had been living in Manhattan as a prostitute and drug dealer. She had slept with some of these men during her time in New York City, they would stipulate; they had given her gifts, bought her meals, thrown her small jobs, helped her pay her rent, etc. – all the standard stuff that big-city bachelors routinely do to keep good-looking starlets interested in them. A few of these snakes, who were no doubt compensated for their time and testimony, also were purportedly ready to testify that on occasion Sherry had given them drugs, or made drugs available to them, or, in effect, slept with them for drugs. In other words, Sherry was going to be made to look like a drug-dealing hooker, irresponsible and amoral, a grifter on the fringe of society, who was living off a man even now. This characterization of Sherry was by way of showing that it was reasonable for Lesewer and Colossal not to have been able to find her, even though her number and her service number were on everything she gave him. There was a side benefit to these allegations: the implication that if this nasty business went public, Sherry's reputation would be ruined.

Colossal Records wanted Sherry to walk away from her name, her original music, and her lyrics. In exchange, they offered her a shot at vocalizing new tunes by writers like Carole Bayer Seger, and would put her together with Teena Marie who was working on: "I'm a Sucker for Your Love." They would give Sherry a contract, and put a group together for her.

Then came another shock to sink the real Sherry's case forever: She had recorded "Better Be Real" with the band of four young guys she put together on the coast. She was relying on those guys, her buddies, to back her up, and add the weight of numbers to her claim. Imagine her shock when she learned that Colossal had signed all the members of her group, given them a new name, and ensured their careers for the next couple of years at least. The guys from Sherry's LA group were in the Colossal stable now, and it was immediately clear that none of them was about to screw up his new-found patron by testifying in Sherry's behalf – convictions and principles be damned.

To add insult to innuendo, Colossal's team told Sherry that if she didn't take their offer, she would never work in the recording business again, for any big label, ever. Evidently, they were confident that they had the power to make this threat a reality, and Sherry's lawyers didn't say anything to dispute the implication.

There was a settlement. Sherry told me it was for two million dollars – her attorneys got half of that. Part of the deal offered by Colossal was that she would relinquish her name and walk away. Part of the deal was that she would shut up about the whole affair, and not run around disclosing the truth. (I heard the story and about Colossal's offer from Sherry before the settlement. After the settlement I never heard from her again.) The thing that amazes me is the record company's arrogance at assuming that they could pull it off. The thing that *really* amazes me is that they **did** pull it off.

Before the settlement, I asked Sherry why she never asked me to help; to testify or submit an affidavit in her behalf, or whatever. She told me, thanks, but she felt I had done enough, and she had tried to keep her friends out of the line of fire. I asked her if there was anything I could do for her now.

"No," she said. "Thanks, but no. It's all over."

"So, who are you now?" I said

"I'm... nobody," she said softly.

* * *

A friend of mine in LA who lived close to Sherry in Marina del Rey told me that after receiving her share of the settlement, Sherry was sitting at an LA crossing in her new Porsche, when she was suddenly T-boned by a cement truck. "Broke every bone in my body," she told my friend, and put her in an ICU on the critical list for weeks. The money she got from the Colossal lawsuit, the money that was left over after her lawyers took their share, was just enough to cover her medical bills and a score of surgeries and plastic surgeries. But the Porsche, like Sherry's music career, was a total loss.

Just as Colossal Records threatened, Sherry never got to work in, for, or through a major recording studio again, ever. Even the jingle people shunned her. Last time I saw her, she told me she was temping in the law offices of the firm that had argued her case. And that she had done some bit voice-over work for Hanna Barbera, like playing Dino, the dog, in The Flintstones. It would have to be something that small and transparent, because no one in the industry would want to offend Colossal Records. I called Hanna Barbera some years later and they said that Sherry had never worked for them.

I went to an Internet music-CD site and looked up Sherry Lund a few days ago, and there she was, the voluminous replacement "Sherry Lund," with a couple of albums, the lead title being *The Best of Sherry Lund*, which keyed on her one and only big single, "Better Be Real." There was another album from England, and one that hyped some duet she did with Luther Vandross. The language on the site was embarrassingly overinflated, and gave the impression that this was a B-list talent that needed all the hype it could get. I ordered the CD on the Web, put the CD in the player and out came the lead tune "Better Be Real." It sounded just like the one the original Sherry had brought to my office to dub, but I suppose the producers could have recreated the tune with new musicians, and the "new" Sherry. All the other tunes on the CD, the ones written and recorded by the replacement Sherry Lund, were so pedestrian that I frankly couldn't bear listening to them. My wife walked into the room and asked, "What's *that*?" And later my daughter, Alex, 28 at the time, asked, "What *in the world* are you listening to?"

One evening in 1998 I walked into my family room and did a double-take: on the tube was a big *Summer Jam '98*. One of the featured talents, "Sherry Lund," was performing "her" big hit tune, "Better Be Real."

Cameras panned through the audience; young people were mouthing the words to the song. Twenty years after it hit, a bunch of people in Jamaica were singing the song – that's how big it was. It was a huge, long-lived hit. Who knows how much money Colossal made off it.

I wondered if the real Sherry Lund, the original one, the eviscerated nonentity who would never work in music again, was sitting somewhere in the world watching the same TV show I was, and what she was feeling.

CHAPTER 6 NIH SYNDROME; NOT INVENTED HERE

My NY production company, Delmar Productions, had been doing low-budget, regional and "test" TV commercials for several years, and we were trying to break into the big-budget arena. The only known way to do this is to develop connections, and use them to get to the high-end jobs. It helped if you were deeply involved socially with the people who could feed you such jobs, and were, incidentally, a generous supplier of their recreational drug of the year; cocaine, hash or pot. I had no connections in this rarefied atmosphere, and no interest in distributing cocaine, hashish or pot so my assault on this market was doomed from the get-go. I was under the influence of the sophomoric delusion that I could gain access to this world via pure talent. Well, c'mon, it could happen. I suppose.

Of course, the first thing I was told was that no one would give me a shot at a full-blown, national, Class-A, commercial until I had produced such a thing. It was a clear case of Catch-22. My solution was just to go out and produce an award-winning commercial for a household-name national consumer product, at my expense. I had another idea; if I produced a spot that was tied into an up-and-coming agency producer, or creative, I could ingratiate myself to him or her in the process. I looked around for a likely up-an-coming agency producer with a pet storyboard or script to produce – one that had been rejected by the client, or by the legal department, or because it was "too creative." (To help you understand the process; an agency producer works for the ad agency, and doesn't actually produce the spot. The outside producer, who works for or owns the production company actually produces the spot. The agency producer's job is to make sure the outside producer doesn't rip the agency off too badly, delivers the job on time, and doesn't go off the charts on some creative extravaganza, or frivolous side-trip. If you're an outside producer, or a director, which I was, part of that job is to befriend, seduce and "take care of" agency producers and Creative Directors with gifts and benefits, like Director's Guild memberships, so they could make a "creative contribution" on the set without breaking some Guild or union regulation.)

One of the agency producers I spoke to was Mort Kallum at an agency then called Ted Bates (subsequently Backer Spielvogel Bates). Mort was, at the time, not one of the "big" producers, and was working to get recognition. His wife, Erika, was a copywriter at another agency. When I told Mort about my idea, he immediately pulled out of his desk a "spec" board he and his wife had done for their portfolio of storyboard samples.

The spot was for Colgate's Cold Power laundry detergent. It showed an Eskimo couple somewhere in an arctic wasteland. The bigger Eskimo is carrying a harpoon, and the shorter one, presumably his mate, has a bag of laundry over her back (this was before Political Correctness, you appreciate). All you would hear would be the Arctic ambiance of high-aspect wind. The Eskimos come to a hole in the ice, kneel down and dump their laundry into the icy water. One sprinkles in a couple of handfuls of Cold Power, and the other stirs the laundry with the back-end of his harpoon. We dissolve to the finished laundry being wringed out and loaded in the sack. The voice-over says, "Cold Power, the colder it gets, the harder it works." We dissolve again to the Eskimo couple dwindling in the distance as they trudge, back, presumably, to their igloo. We hear the distant howl of a lone bachelor wolf as a white-out punctuates the scene.

"Won't the clothes sink when they throw them in the hole?" I ask.

"I don't know. Ask Erika," says Mort.

"Is she an Eskimo?" I ask.

"Please," says Mort.

"I love the spot," I say. "I'll do it."

"What do you mean, you'll do it?"

"I'll produce it."

"But, Ken, it was only a portfolio board. No one will pay to produce this."

"Out of my own pocket."

"You know it'll never go anywhere."

"I know. I want it for my reel, to show that I can do a full-fledged national spot."

"Fine, but I think you're nuts," says Kallum. "You know what it would cost to produce a spot like this? Location scouting, casting, traveling, hazardous-duty pay, the special equipment for the cold. Dealing with SAG. Costume, makeup, crew and equipment, everything falling through the ice. Insurance. Transportation up into snow country, lodging... Sheesh. Fuggedaboudit."

"I'm gonna do it."

"Okay. Knock yourself out."

"I'm thinking of a place in Vermont, a friend's farm. This time of year it's like the Artic. I'm going to shoot this up there in, like, two weekends from now. You and Erika are welcome to come?"

"You're totally insane."

"It's my best feature."

"Thanks, Kenny, but we're going on vacation. Florida Keys. You can freeze your ass off in God-forsaken arctic Vermont. Good luck, pal."

I called Judd Fischer, my best college buddy and oldest friend, in North Pomfret, Vermont, and told him what I planned to do. I asked him if I could bring this friend of mine up on the weekend to play the Eskimo. The friend was a big, handsome Chinese guy named Howard Toy. Howard was dating our baby-sitter. He was bright and friendly and I liked him a lot. Howard would make a great Eskimo. I was off the storyboard already, which called for a couple, but I thought it would work better with a lone Eskimo and since no one was paying me to do the spot, and I was the producer, plus the director, not to mention the cameraman, assistant camera, grip, ice handler, location scout, casting director, driver, production assistant, and editor. I had free-reign.

The Fischer farm had a nice pond not far from the house. It was a man-made pond, to provide water for the livestock, so although it was almost as big as a football field, it wasn't very deep. Maybe four feet at the deepest point. This was important, because if Howard or I, or both of us went through the ice, it would facilitate getting out alive if we could stand on the bottom.

My friend Judd was a sculptor, and had welding equipment, with which he made a harpoon out of rebar. He also had a huge old raccoon coat, and great furry boots that looked like they were Eskimo-made. We swiped a fur hood from an old coat. We put all this stuff on Howard, plus a pair of heavy, old leather gloves, and we had our Eskimo. An inside-out burlap feed-sack became the laundry sack, and we filled it with discarded clothes from the Fischer's rag bin. A battered, old hatchet completed our Eskimo's gear.

I went out on the iced-over lake with Howard, just the two of us because we didn't know if the ice was thick enough to carry anyone else. My wife and Judd stayed on the shore, with a wooden ladder and a length of rope standing by in case Howard or I or both of us went through the ice. There was a slope of pure, white snow behind the pond, and I framed my shots with this in the background, and overexposed slightly so it would completely white out, like an arctic winter sky.

I directed Howard, with the sack of laundry over his shoulder and his harpoon in the other, to wander across the ice and poke occasionally as if looking for a fault in the surface. I followed him with a hand-held Bell & Howell 16mm Filmo camera, the US workhorse combat camera of WWII.

Howard The Eskimo discovers a fault in the ice, puts down his sack of laundry and starts picking out a hole in the ice with his harpoon. He gets down on one knee, pulls out his hatchet, and cuts a manhole size hunk out of the ice. When the disk of ice is free, he reaches into the crack on both sides and lifts it out of the hole. He slides the disk of ice clear of the hole. Neither of us knew how thick the ice was, or if it would be possible to do this, but there it was. I guess if you're an Eskimo and you have a sack of laundry to do, you find a way to get to the water. The hole Howard had made wasn't filled with nice, clear water, but icy slush the consistency of a 7-11 Slushie.

"If I throw the laundry in, it's gonna sink," said Howard between takes.

"Toss it in and see what happens," I replied. That's all we could do. "Maybe sort of keep it near the top by stirring it with your hatchet handle."

So, Howard threw the laundry in the hole, and stirred it a bit with his hatchet. And it didn't sink! I suppose the slush held it up. I shot this experiment as it happened.

"It's not sinking," says Howard, as amazed as I. "Stop talking. Follow the script, I'm rolling," says I, my frozen fingers starting to act a bit sluggishly on the camera controls. So Howard becomes an Eskimo again. He puts down his hatchet, opens his sack and pulls out a large box of Cold Power. He opens the box top and pours out a handful of detergent and sprinkles it over his laundry. Then he picks up his harpoon and stirs the laundry around in the slush – and the clothes stay near the surface! Soapsuds form on the surface. Oh my god, this stuff actually does work in cold water.

After a few shots of Howard stirring the laundry, he pulls it out, wrings it out and loads it, and the box of Cold Power back into the sack. He gets up and hefts the sack of laundry over his shoulder. He picks up his harpoon and starts trudging away from me at a slight angle, off into the endless whiteness, presumably back to his igloo. It really looked like the middle of snow and ice-covered nowhere. There was no trace of the trees, or the farm over the swell.

I took the exposed footage back to my New York office, sent it to Movielab for processing, and post-produced it. That is, I did the editing, set up the work print for the optical effects, which were several dissolves, and laid in the sound effects. I had shot a total of one hundred feet of 16mm film, or a total of three minutes, against a finished spot of thirty seconds. Everything had worked out brilliantly. The exposures were all perfect, which is always a challenge in a snowy winter environment. Howard was great, a natural. His outfit and gear were totally convincing. Nanook of the North, with a touch of Zen. The fact that the laundry didn't sink in the icy slush was a serendipity I still don't understand, but I'm sure any Eskimo who washes his own clothes through a hole in the ice could explain it to me.

My father, for decades a top radio announcer and voice-over talent, did the voice-over. He intones: "Cold Power – the colder it gets, the harder it works," as the Eskimo puts his sack of laundry on his back, and heads off into the arctic wasteland. I ended the audio track with this haunting bachelor wolf call I got for free from the Museum of Natural History.

When I was done, and the finished answer print came back from Movielab, I had produced, for a grand total of four hundred and sixty five dollars, the coolest, purest, greatest TV spot ever made, and I'm not kidding.

I had worked at McCann-Erickson, a NY advertising for a couple of years right out of college, so I knew the politics of the agency-client relationship, and the existence of the NIH syndrome (Not Invented Here), so I knew not to run out and send the spot directly to Colgate. I found out which ad agency handled Cold Power, and sent it to them. It was Norman, Craig and Kummel, (NC&K) and the TV producer on the account was a guy named Joe Lamneck. I sent him a print of the spot, and enclosed a letter stating that what I hoped for was a chance to bid on some of NC&K's upcoming TV spots. I called him a week later to follow-up the letter, and talked with an assistant who put me off. After a few weeks of calling I finally got Mr. Lamneck to take my call. He and a couple of his associates at NC&K had screened the spot, he said, and found it "cute," but "not effective advertising," which is what they told the ad director of the product at Colgate.

There was no point disagreeing with Lamneck and his associates. NC&K's reputation as an agency was clearly anti-creative; if anything, they were proud of it. They were well-established as the dullest agency in New York, even duller than Ted Bates, which prided itself for years on being astoundingly dull. NC&K's philosophy, was virtually identical to that espoused by German propagandists of the late thirties and early forties; to push the product relentlessly and saturate the market, until everyone was sick of it, and keep repeating their message ad nauseam. NC&K's founder and longtime chief executive was a man named Norman Norman. Consistent with NC&K's lack of originality, his parents couldn't even think up an original first name for him.

Having been formally rejected and belittled by NC&K, I now felt I had the moral right to approach the client directly. But first I wanted a little more credibility than having produced what I and my colleagues, friends and relatives thought was the greatest commercial ever made, so I submitted the spot to two of the leading creative awards organizations in Manhattan. They were both hot, prestigious award competitions. I won them both, the top award in the category in each case, and I won more awards for categories I didn't even enter! One of the organizations called and asked if they could include the spot in their international Ten Best Commercials of the Year. Sure, I said. I sent copies of the awards to NC&K, and a note, suggesting that the spot was something more than "cute," and asking once again if they would pass it on to Colgate, or at least bid us on upcoming spots. Naturally, I got no reply.

I made a couple of calls and found out that the ad director at Colgate in charge of Cold Power was a man named Sandy Haver. I sent a 16mm print of the spot to Mr. Haver's office, along with a letter stating that I hoped he liked it, and that my goal was to be given an opportunity to bid on the production of upcoming spots, or industrial films they were thinking about doing. I got no reply, so after a couple of weeks I called Mr. Haver's office, and used a ruse to get through. When I mentioned the Cold Power Eskimo spot, a light went on. "Oh, yes," he said, "the people at NC&K showed me that. They said it was made by a film student."

"Student?" I said, my dander rising. "Not quite. I worked in broadcast writing and production for McCann Erickson for three years, and I've been producing TV spots in New York for four years. My company..."

"Well, that's great, Ken. I loved the spot, but the NC&K people told me it wasn't effective advertising, and they're the experts."

"Do you know what 'not effective advertising' means, Mr. Haver? Everyone who's seen it loves the spot. It just won *seven* awards. It won awards in categories I didn't even enter it in. Did the people at NC&K tell you why they thought it was 'not effective advertising?'"

"Sorry, Ken, I can't really get into this with you now, because I'm taking a leave of absence to work on the McGovern campaign, and I'm packing up my desk as we speak. But, good luck with your career, okay?"

"Yes, thank you, Mr. Haver. And good luck with your McGovern campaign. Hopefully it will have more imagination than your pathetically boring and hugely pedestrian Cold Power spots." No, you're right, I didn't say that last part. I should have, but I didn't, because you don't burn any bridges unless you absolutely have to.

That was the end of the brilliant career of my fantastic Cold Power commercial. NC&K predictably ragged on it, because they hadn't come up with anything as good for the entire history of the agency, and the man at Colgate didn't have the time or whatever it would take to go over his agency's head.

You can understand NC&K's reaction when you consider that ad agencies at the time made their money almost exclusively from the 15% margin discount they got from media, so the only edge they could offer over any other agency was their brilliant creative talent. My walking in from the outside and producing a spot that made their best stuff look like a cheap wedding video from Fargo, North Dakota, didn't make them look good at all. I don't know what Mr. Haver's excuse was, except that he was mentally off on the political campaign, or he didn't trust his own judgment, or he didn't want to rock the boat. One doesn't know what relationships and scenarios are in place behind the scenes. Maybe Haver didn't want to step on someone's toes, or disturb an existing connection, or call attention to himself by breaking a traditional pattern of behavior. Or maybe he was just temporarily brain-dead from having swum through the endless flood of perpetual pabulum from NC&K.

Years later a Cold Power TV spot aired that featured a large polar bear rearing up on its hind legs as the announcer railed on about the remarkable features and benefits of Cold Power, but the bear wasn't doing his laundry, and there was no Eskimo in sight. The stupid Polar Bear spot was at least ten times "less effective" than my Eskimo spot. I'm sure millions of people across America saw this polar bear piece of crap week after week and wondered what the dopey bear had to do with doing your laundry. Oh, right, bears live where it's cold, whoopdeedoo. I guess the agency people who produced this derivative piece of dreck were worried that I, or Mort Kallum and his wife, would have hired a lawyer and gone after them if they had used an Eskimo doing his laundry through a hole in the ice. And I would have, too.

I sent Mort a couple of prints of the spot, so he could put it on his own reel, and give one to his wife, Erika, to put on hers. I met with Mort at his office later, and he told me his wife was so disgusted with the ad business that she had quit, and never wanted to work as an advertising copywriter again. Mort couldn't believe that I was able to produce the spot for $465. But he never gave me a chance to bid on any of the full-blown national spots he worked on later. I guess he didn't have the power to make such a wild and reckless decision. He would have to continue to use the same old guys approved by the Big Producers in power.

My Cold Power Eskimo spot is still the greatest detergent spot ever made, and right up there with the best commercials of all time. What a shame that no one at NC&K had the courage to say, "Hey, this is fantastic, why didn't we think of that? How much would you like to sell the spot to us right now?" Or, "This is huge. How would you like a job here, kid?" Or, anything other than their thinly-veiled weasel effort to make the spot go away by calling it "cute," or a "student film," or "ineffective advertising." And what a shame that no one at Colgate had the guts or imagination to say, "Hey, nuts to NC&K -- this is terrific, this is clearly the best, most original goddam thing anyone ever did for this product. So what if it didn't come from our agency, let's just ask the kid what he wants for the thing Let's make a deal with him and buy the spot and get it on the air and sell tons more Cold Power than we ever sold before, goddammit." I would have sold the spot for a lousy thousand dollars, or even at cost, or even just given it to them, if they would have just said "Great work, kid," or maybe just let me bid on a few upcoming spots.

CHAPTER 7   AT LEAST YOUR FRIENDS WON'T SCREW YOU.

My wife, Ulli, a Realtor, was a buyer's broker for a young couple she had been showing houses to for a couple of months. The couple were pre-qualified for a mortgage, knew just what they wanted, and were going to hold out until they found what they were looking for. Ulli found their dream house, they made an offer, Ulli and the sellers' broker negotiated back and forth until they came to a mutually agreeable price, and just before they went to contract, another buyer came along and got the house for full price.

The couple was very disappointed and Ulli went back on the hunt. After a while she found another perfect house, which happened to belong to a friend of mine, who I had known for some years, and with whom I occasionally played tennis. He wasn't evidently a good enough friend to give my wife the listing, but we attributed this to his wife, who was a born-and-bred Southerner, who loathed Yankees and couldn't wait to move back to Dixieland. So we assumed his wife insisted on giving the listing to someone who better suited her Southern sensitivities.

The young house-hunting couple loved the second perfect house, made an offer, and negotiations began between Ulli and the sellers' agent. During the negotiations, Ulli had to go out of town for one day and asked an associate, an agent in her office, to cover for her. After she returned the listing broker had to leave town for a couple of days, and a stand-in from her office acted in her behalf. The negotiations matured and a figure was agreed upon between buyers and sellers. Ulli already had a binder from the buyers, and the binder check in hand, so all she needed was for the seller, my good friend, to deliver the counter-signed contract.

My friend told Ulli on the phone that evening that the contract was already signed, and he'd fax it to her in the morning. She offered to drive over and pick it up right away, since he was only a couple of miles away. But it was already early evening, and he said it wasn't necessary, and he'd fax it that night to our home if she needed it so fast. Fine, said Ulli.

Well, it never came that night, and the next morning Ulli missed him before he left for work, and when she called him at work, he was in a meeting. The meeting went on and on, until the day was over, and my friend, the would-be seller, never called back.

Ulli called the listing broker's stand-in at her office, and her home, but couldn't reach her, and she never called back either. Ulli, now beginning to worry, called the seller's home a few more times that evening, and got the runaround. Ulli's young buyers were ringing the phone off the hook wondering what the hell was wrong. Did they have a house or not? Finally the original listing agent returned and called Ulli to tell her she was sorry, but the sellers had decided to sell to another couple who had offered five thousand more for the house. Ulli was stunned. Who was the selling broker, she asked? The listing broker reluctantly revealed that it was the agent Ulli had asked to pinch hit for her the day she was out of town.

This man knew exactly where the deal was, and that the contract hadn't been signed, and he brought in his own customers behind Ulli's back, and made an offer five thousand higher than Ulli's people had negotiated. The seller, my, uh, friend, didn't say anything to Ulli because he wanted to make the extra five thousand dollars. Ulli's associate at her office, who she trusted, didn't say anything to her, of course, because he wanted to sabotage her deal and push through his own. The agent who was pinch-hitting for the out-of-town listing agent didn't say anything to Ulli because the seller, my friend, told her to deal with the rat from Ulli's office who had gone behind her back. And also, because the back-up listing agent was new, and didn't know quite what to do, she maintained her silence.

So the sneaky deal proceeded apace without Ulli or her customers having any idea their deal had been sidetracked. When the young couple learned their second house had been yanked out of their grasp, they walked away in frustration and disgust, feeling somehow that Ulli was to blame for their misfortune. So she lost the deal, and her clients. The people involved in the ambush deal hadn't done anything actually illegal, it was just dirty pool, and the shabbiest kind of sleaze.

Predictably, the parties who facilitated the back-door deal, especially the associate from her own office, frantically tried to make excuses and do damage control, because they knew that sometime down the road, they would need a favor from Ulli, or she would be in a position one day to screw them. What goes around comes around. Unfortunately, Ulli isn't the kind of woman who holds a grudge until she can take revenge – she's just not that kind of person. The saddest comment on the sleazoid rats that pulled the ambush deal is that they knew that about Ulli going in.

* * *

But wait, there's an ironic, positive postscript. I was still in touch with my "friend," on another business front. I was sitting in a meeting with him in his office a few weeks after the bum real estate deal closed, and in passing told him that I had heard that Ulli and her customers were upset because my so-called friend and his agents closed precipitously without giving them a chance to make a higher offer. This young couple, Ulli's customers, were a doctor and a nurse, they loved the house, they had the money, and they would have raised the stakes another ten thousand, or more, just like that.

The expression on my friend's face was wonderful: he and his ambush agents and customers had pushed the deal through

74

fast and under the radar without saying anything to Ulli because they were ashamed of what they were doing. They were so busy pulling a fast one for a lousy extra five grand that it never occurred to them that they could have made ten grand more, or even more than that, from the people they were so busy screwing.

My friend immediately called his attorney in front of me and asked if he couldn't sue the listing broker for not contacting Ulli and telling her that he was going to sell the house to someone else for more money, and giving her people a chance to raise their offer. The lawyer didn't think they had a snowball's chance in hell at winning such a suit, since my friend had been in the driver's seat on the ambush deal, and had instructed the listing agent's assistant to deal with the back-stabber. Ooops.

CHAPTER 8   THE GOAL OF A COMPANY IS TO PROSPER

A well-fixed friend of my father's, let's call him Dave, owned an anodizing plant in Long Island City, New York. Well, he owned it, but the corporation registration papers showed the CEO and majority stockholder as one of Dave's sons. The son was eighteen, just starting college, and had nothing to do with dad's business. I was a year younger, 17, and I worked at Dave's anodizing company for three months before I went off to college, so I got to witness and participate in this story first-hand.

Anodizing is a process in which metals are colored, or coated with a finish for esthetics, functionality, or durability. Dave, a successful entrepreneur, had owned six other anodizing businesses before this one. Each one of the previous firms had gone bankrupt, and Dave made good money each time. Here's how it worked:

Dave didn't consciously engineer the profitable bankruptcy of his company the first time it happened; it was accidental. When business turned sour and the end was about to come, Dave had a bunch of important jet engine parts currently in the plant, being treated with a process called Martin Hardcoat, which imparts a very hard and durable surface. The parts were from one of the major aeronautics manufacturers, Lockheed, Boeing, Republic... I forget which. The major manufacturer was already behind schedule on a huge contract, and had to have its anodized parts back ASAP. And here's poor Dave going castors up. When he declared he was insolvent, or filed for bankruptcy, the judge would put a freeze on all inventory. Everything in the place would be deadlined until supervisors could be put in place, auditors would audit, lawyers could wrangle, inspectors could inspect, and God knows what other interminable hoohah would have to take place before Lockheed, or whoever, could get their urgent, precious parts back.

Dave felt sorry for his good contact and old friend at the aviation firm, so he called him the night before he went castors up and made a proposal. It went something like this:

"Sam, it's Dave. Listen, we're in big trouble here. The bank just called our loan, and there's no way I can pay it. Two or three days and I'm going into receivership, or whatever the hell the lawyers tell me to do."

"Jesus Christ, Dave, *what about our parts!*"

"That's why I'm calling, bud. Your job is about twenty five percent done, okay? I'd feel really lousy if your parts got sucked into this bottomless whirlpool of Chapter 11 or insolvency bullshit, so here's my idea. It'll be a few days before they send in the marshals and the suits to lock everything up. I can call in every man I know, set up three shifts, work around the clock, and get your job out of here in three days. We'll load directly into the trucks and my boys and I'll drive the trucks under the radar directly to your plant each night."

"Jeez, Dave, you think you can make it?"

"Yeah, I do."

"What if you get busted and they impound our parts?"

"No one's going to bust us, Sam. We got three or four days before the axe falls."

"If I don't get those parts..."

"I'm going to take care of you, Sam. Only thing, I'm sorry, but it's going to cost you. It's going to cost big, you know, for the overtime."

"Right, right. I understand."

"I could go to jail for this, Sam. And my guys with me. Figure a premium of around three, three times the contract. And that's cash, Sam. It's gotta be off the books and under the table. Can you make it happen?"

"You mean three times your original bid?"

"Right. Anything over that, I'll eat. And cash, COD, Sam. The auditors and the suits can't ever see this money. This is strictly between you and me, understand?"

"I'll get it. No problem"

"You can break the cash into thirds and pay me part each night, so you're only paying for what you get."

"Deal. Listen, Dave, thanks. I know you're sticking your neck out here, and I appreciate what you're doing, buddy."

"Hey, I'm going to do what I can for my old friend and best customer."

And so, Dave shafts his old friend and best customer, makes a bundle of cash, tax free, burns his creditors, and whistles while he walks. Now, don't go away angry – there's an up-side: Dave really is a mensch at heart: he doesn't let his workers go. He doesn't have to, because he knows the anodizing business, he's cash rich, and he knows how to be up and running again in a couple of weeks at a new site a quarter of a mile away. He uses his workers to set up the next plant. Of course, because he went bankrupt, he can't be the majority share-holder of another corporation for seven years, so he names his wife. And for the next corporation, his oldest son. Then the next son. Then his daughter. Then his mother, and so on. And each time he goes bankrupt, the plant just happens to have in process a large and important order of parts belonging to a deep-pockets manufacturer. And each time Dave is such a decent guy that he saves this customer's ass by working around the clock and spiriting the order out under cover of night in a week or less. One customer was so impressed by Dave's old-world morality and work ethic that he went through this process twice! That's right, ladies and gentlemen, twice Dave saved him from Dave, and twice the unsuspecting mark thanked Dave for doing it.

CHAPTER 9   DO A JOB AS PROMISED, AND YOU'LL BE PAID

My company produced a number of TV commercials and radio spots for a medium-size New York ad agency. The agency was dragging its feet egregiously on the issue of payment and I had to nag them more and more vociferously, which activity I loathe. When most of the invoices moved into the 90 days and over column, I threatened legal action. Finally, the CEO of the agency called me and my producer in for a meeting to discuss the outstanding invoices. I wanted to ask, "What's to discuss," but I bit my tongue and focused on getting all the back-up materials together that we would use to substantiate our invoices – as if there was any question.

But of course, legally there is. If you send someone a bill and they contest it, they have rights. One gets up in arms about this silliness, until one is the recipient of an incorrect or unjust bill, and then one is all in favor of the rights of the billee.

My staff producer at the time was a New Yorker, a tough bird who had been around the block and knew where all the potholes were. She was of the same background as the agency CEO, so I figured it would be smart to strategize with her and involve her in the meeting as well. I took her into the meeting both to back me up and to signal me if I was going overboard in one direction or another, which I have been known to do when I am overcome with righteous indignation.

The two of us went to this meeting at the agency, and were met in the conference by four people from the recalcitrant firm. Already we were on the low end of the playing field: we were in their ballpark, and we were outnumbered two to one. Next to the agency president was the bookkeeper, and flanking them were the account executive and the creative director who had ordered most of the stuff we did. The agency director opened the meeting, and outlined the agenda.

We went through each job we did and action we performed to contract completion, blow by blow, looking at each item, when and how it was done, when it was approved, delivered and invoiced, etc. The total due us, by the way, was some sixty thousand dollars. Every so often an item came up that left the tiniest bit of wiggle room, and the agency people would wiggle right in and try to make a big deal out of nothing. But we hung tough and refused to surrender just because they wanted us to surrender.

After a half day of this pain, when my producer and I were starting to get exhausted from resisting the wheedling and hair-splitting, the CEO glommed onto something like a moray eel and wouldn't let us wrap up, shake hands and go back to our offices.. It was something to do with a piece of original music that we had estimated would cost five thousand dollars, but the final invoice was for $5,900.00. Mr. CEO for the agency didn't want to pay the additional nine hundred. I pointed out that the composer/arranger had requested to add two additional instruments to his orchestration, and that he had, before the recording session, requested the additional money for the musicians and additional studio time, and that the request had been passed on to and approved by the agency creative director. But the CEO said he had not been consulted, and the creative guy started working hard to make it look like I had twisted his arm to approve the overage. It started to get ugly. To break the tension, we all agreed on a ten minute break for coffee and pit stops.

My producer caught me in the hallway and whispered, "You got to give him something or he looks like he lost in front of his people. Split it with him on the nine hundred and he'll happily pay you the sixty thou. But make it look like it's killing you. Like he's taking food out of the mouths of your children."

We went back into the meeting and I played this role. I bemoaned the fate of my near-starving children. I twisted and groaned and put my hands on my head. I settled for only half of the nine hundred in question, goddammit, and you should have seen the tension seep out of the room like air out of a punctured beach ball. We left the agency conference room with a check for $59,550.00, which was a whole hell of a lot more than we would have gotten if I had refused to let them beat me out of *something*.

*　*　*

When I send out an invoice these days, and a check comes back for the amount in full in under thirty days, I am shocked, dazzled, flabbergasted. It's such an anomaly I feel like sending a thank-you note. But I don't because it was probably a mistake.

CHAPTER 10   PEOPLE WILL RESPECT YOUR CONVICTIONS

I was called by the Manhattan manager of a world-class rock star to drop by the brownstone they owned in Greenwich Village and bid on package of three TV spots, a couple of radio lifts, and related print ads for an upcoming album. This manager heard that I was winning awards for my creative film work, and when he called a couple of friends to vet me, they must have had good things to say. I can't tell you the name of the rock star or his group, because that would result in immediate lawsuits brought by expensive lawyers, which I don't have the time, patience or disposable income to deal with. For the sake of brevity, let's just call the group, and its lead singer, "Warpaint."

The theme of Warpaint's new album (you have to have a theme; good music isn't enough) was, let's say, blowing up the

Pentagon. Warpaint's manager messengered me a one-off copy of the tunes, and some text that had been prepared by the Warpaint marketing staff and publicist. The manager, Bob (not his real name), called and told me he wanted to see me in a week with scripts, boards and production cost estimates. I asked him what the budget parameters were, to see if I was really in the running, and he told me, "around a million." Fine. I could do that. A million would be just fine. This was New York City, the Big-time. It could happen. It happened every day.

I called a meeting and my staff and I went to work immediately on coming up with a kickass concept, and then capturing and conveying it dramatically in presentation media. To put the presentation together cost me about four thousand dollars, including the outstanding storyboard artist I hired for the occasion, and the production of a sample rough-cut of stock scenes I called a swipe-o-matic.

A week later I showed up at the Warpaint brownstone, my material in hand, and rang the doorbell. It was one in the afternoon, as I recall, and I hadn't eaten any lunch because I wanted to be maximally sharp for my presentation.

The girl-angel of perhaps eighteen who opened the door was the most beautiful girl I had ever seen in the flesh. She had lovely, long hair, not brown, but not blonde, and large, limpid pale blue eyes. I fell in love with her in about 0.7 seconds. She led me into a small but nicely decorated waiting room. There were photos on the wall of Warpaint concerts, a bunch of gold and platinum records, and three or four guitars smashed onstage by the Chief of Warpaint.

The young adorable angel seemed to be in some sort of trance. When I spoke to her, it took a couple of seconds before there was any sign of reaction or mental process in her eyes. Then she would answer me very carefully and slowly, like she had a speech impediment and didn't want to misspeak herself. It's as if she was underwater and running at half-slow motion, or, alternatively, she may have been a test model of a sex robot. But she was so beautiful it didn't matter. She could have been an inflatable party doll, and you still would have had to fall in love with her.

I sat in the waiting room for about five minutes when the door opened and a second young woman appeared. This one was a bit older, say maybe twenty three or four. She was a dark-eyed brunette with soft wavy hair, boudoir eyes, the most luscious mouth imaginable, a remarkable body, and unblemished, white skin.

"Hi, Ken," she said, honey in her teeth, "follow me." Definitely. I would have followed her up the Matterhorn, or down to the river Styx. In less than 0.5 of a second, I had fallen out of love with the first girl, and was now irretrievably in love with this slinky paragon of gorgeousity. I followed her undulating loins up a flight of stairs, wishing that it would go on for a few hundred additional yards, then down a short hallway, and into Bob's office. The smoldering brunette left me at the door, carrying off my heart with her. Bob was on the phone. He gestured for me to take a seat at the other side of his imposing, glass over marquetry-topped desk.

While Bob chatted on the phone I thought about the beautiful girls and women who attach themselves to rock musicians. What's the attraction? I wondered. Don't these gaga groupies take a split second to consider what they are getting themselves into before they jump in a stretch limo and administer the Monica to some grungy roach who doesn't know their name or even care to know it? No, these pathetic women come straight from the maw of the monster of mosh pit mass hypnosis. Have you ever seen them in the flesh? The insane, mindless covetousness in their eyes as they scream and writhe and yearn with every fiber of their being to be possessed and used by some hirsute, low-class ignoramus with dirty fingernails who can strum a guitar and whine unintelligibly. These pathetic groupies see and hear and feel the females around them doing the same thing, screaming, drooling, trying to clamber onstage to touch the object of their, what, madness? What do these women expect? After an hour or two of anonymous sex, or a few days or weeks of riding around in a bus, being passed around by members of the band, and then by the roadies, they are painfully rejected. Or, at best, the really good-lookers end up doing stupid jobs for the band or its entourage, strung out on dope, sexual objects for whoever in the entourage has the time and energy to poke their pudendas.

As I sat there thinking about the strangeness of the rock groupie, and trying to figure out how to get one of my own, my eyes settled on a pile of white stuff sitting on top of Bob's glass-topped desk. The powdery mountain rising from it was about seven inches tall and a foot wide. What could it be? I spotted a couple of single-edge razor blades next to the mountain of white, and a crystal shot-glass with an assortment of silver and gold straws in it. Ah ha, so I was looking at a mountain of coke, boys and girls. What would so much coke be worth? I had no idea. One hundred thousand? Five hundred thousand? Did this mean that if I accidently sneezed the crest off the top of Mt. Snow it could cost Bob about $25,000?

The door behind me opened. I turned and witnessed the entrance of a fully grown, woman of perhaps 28, a wrenchingly perfect celestial goddess. She was blonde, and tall, had a perfect model's face, stunning legs and perfect hands and teeth. She made the other two girls look like warmed-over appetizers. I fell in love for the third time. The celestial goddess smiled and asked me, I think, if I wanted some coffee or tea. This woman, who was, I believe, Bob's executive admin, had to perform some actual clerical work, so she was required to have a functioning brain and a skill set. She probably was not a left-over groupie, and probably had been actually hired for the job. She spoke at almost normal speed, but she was moving, like the other girls before her, at some fractional slow-motion setting.

"Hamina... abba... abba..." I sputtered, having completely lost all motor functions and capacity to verbalize at the very sight of her.

"Excuse me," said the goddess, leaning closer, her perfect breasts trying to leap from her perfect silk blouse onto my lap.

"He said yes," said Bob, hanging up his phone. "Coffee, regular. And bring us some clean snoots, babe."

The blonde goddess nodded, turned and left the room.

"Delmar," said Bob, extending his hand across the desk. I took it and shook it.

"Bob," I said, confidently.

"Have you got some great creative for me today, or what?"

"Yes, I do," I said, reaching for my presentation materials.

"Whoa, old paint," said Bob, holding up a hand. "Take your time, dude. We haven't bonded yet."

"Ah," said I. "Right."

"Kick back, rap a bit, see how you roll – shit like that."

"Right. Fine. Bond away."

The breathtaking blonde reentered carrying a champagne flute with about a half dozen swizzle sticks in it. Well, they looked like swizzle sticks at first. When she put the flute down in front of me, I could see that they were nose nozzles.

"Choose your weapon," said Bob. He selected a gold straw with a filigree design on the shaft, and inserted one end of it well up his left nostril. He leaned forward and poised the other end over the awesome volcano of coke on his desk. He inhaled, long and slow, and dug a nice mogul in the side of the alabaster mountain. He put the straw back in the shot glass, cleaned his nose with a Kleenex, and discarded it in the waste basket beneath his desk. He looked up at me as his eyebrows slid high up on his forehead.

"Dive in," he urged.

"Uh... I, uh..."

"You, uh, what?" Bob said, one of his eyebrows digging down toward his nose. "Take a snort, dude."

"Jeez, I don't know, Bob," said I. "I just went through a lot to get away from this."

"You're fulla shit," said Bob, somehow seeing through my ruse. I thought I'd shift gears and try the truth.

"Look, Bob, do you mind if I do my presentation first, and then get stoned?"

"Yeah, I do. Why should I sit here, stoned, and listen to you make a presentation, straight? That won't cut it."

"Well, I frankly don't think I'd do the presentation half as well if I were stoned. I'd leave stuff out, and..."

"Hey, Kenny listen – I never do anything important without getting good and fucked up first. If you can't operate behind a coupla snorts, maybe what you're doing isn't worth doing. Maybe it isn't honest and true."

"No, this is good creative. This is very, very good. Totally honest and true. You're gonna love it."

"Are you telling me you don't trust yourself to show me your stuff unless you're straight?"

"Um, basically, yeah."

"Well, I am stoned, so how can I know good from bad?"

"Good question. I don't know. You'll have to trust me."

"Kenny, I just came back from the Pentagon. Room fulla generals. Piece o' cake. Went to DC for another meeting, to the Treasury Department. Needed clearance to shoot a shitload of real US currency for a cover. Room fulla special agents. Stoned out of my gourd. No problem. Got what I wanted from these guys. They had no idea I was stoned, but I sure could tell they were straight. I'm always massively fucked up when I do business. That's how I see through the shit."

"You mean, like, in vino veritas?"

"Exactly."

"Well, I'm glad that works for you, but I'm not so good when I'm whacked, so, if you don't mind..."

"But I do mind."

"My staff and I worked hard on this. I'd really like to show it to you."

"Sorry, I have to... be somewhere."

"Wait...Really?"

"Uh huh. Goodbye." Bob buzzed for the blonde.

"Should I leave these with you?" I asked, looking at my presentation portfolio.

"No point, really," said Bob. The door opened and the Great White Goddess appeared. Bob picked up his phone and started punching in a number as he swiveled away from the despicable sight of me, probably an undercover agent for the DEA. I picked up my portfolio. The goddess held the door open for me. I tried to catch her eye, but she was carefully looking away. Somehow she could tell that I was an intruder, a "straight" that had refused to snort freely offered nose candy. Definitely a Narc.

So there went that million dollar deal, shafted beyond repair, and no likelihood of being called in on any future projects. But my pride and my honor were intact. Yeah, I still had that, and that. Yeah.

I went back to the office and told my staff what had happened. They sympathized, but they probably left the room thinking, "What is wrong with this jagoff? How are we ever going to make the big-time with this fuckin' straight-arrow square at the helm?"

* * *

For those of you blithe idealists who believe in karma, I'll pass on this postscript: Bob the manager/dope dealer is now a successful Hollywood producer, and is surrounded by even more beautiful women who ask how high when he says jump. He makes ninety three gazillion dollars a year for being a totally self-indulgent hedonist and staying massively stoned all the livelong day, and I'm here slaving away on this book for months at a clip until I'm half blind and my hands are cramped and arthritic. It's a good thing I'm a basically happy person is all I can say.

CHAPTER 11   LEARN EVERY DETAIL ABOUT YOUR BUSINESS

W hen I decided, in my middle teens, that I wanted to work in the motion picture industry, I set out to learn as much as I could about the personnel, the process, the crafts and equipment involved. I read everything I could, especially on directing and the technique of the camera. I also studied audio recording, lighting, camera movement, boom and dolly technique, electric (gaffer), color, makeup, editing, optical effects, audio mixing, etc. I worked whenever I could, doing whatever they'd let me, for free, as a trainee, or whatever.

I schlepped heavy cables, learned how to tie in to the mains, learned how to light a set, how to diffuse, shape and manipulate light. I learned how to load magazines, change lenses, pull focus, check the gate for hairs, jury-rig this and improvise that. I worked on sets ranging from one-man, no-budget student films to big features; loading, assisting the cameraman, operating, recording audio, holding the boom mike, dressing cable, gophering, ("Go for this. Go for that...") working as a grip, gaffer, lighting director. I began to focus on shooting more than audio and post-production. I thought it was important to know as much as I could about every major camera I might be called upon to operate: Arriflex, Eclair, Mitchell, Aaton, Bolex, B&H Filmo and Eymo; and for video, Sony Betacam, Ikegami, JVC and Panasonic. I knew the Arri, Eclair, Bolex and Filmo cameras inside and out, and felt I was a more valuable filmmaker for my fascination and expertise with equipment, how it worked, and how to troubleshoot problems.

But when I got out of the Army and started my own production company, I was a producer. I was the boss, and it was my job to bring in work, not to change a faulty spring in a Mitchell magazine. My job was to go out and sell, to induce corporations and advertisers to use us to make their TV spots, news-films, sponsored programs, sales films, etc. But I thought it was important for me to keep up my skills as a shooter and knowledge of developments in cinematography and videography, so I spent hours reading, playing with our equipment, looking at new stuff at trade shows, shooting when I should have, could have, hired a shooter.

The message was delivered forcefully one afternoon when a cameraman who worked for me asked me if he could take a couple of days off to shoot some screen tests for Carlo Ponti. He also asked if he could borrow my Arri BL camera, and a

Nagra tape recorder. No problem, I said, in an effort to be a nice guy. I volunteered to be the assistant cameraman for two reasons; To keep an eye on my equipment, and to meet Ponti and maybe Sophia Loren as well. Ponti was in New York looking at locations for an upcoming east coast picture, and doing some screen tests of New York actors for supporting roles in the picture. Sophia was in town with him, and also with her new baby, (a big deal after four miscarriages) and she would probably be dropping by at some point. You may wonder how come my employee, Rick Carrier, was friends with Carlo Ponti, and I was not. Rick had met Ponti through Joe Levine, founder of Embassy pictures, which had distributed, in the US, Vittorio Di Sica's *Two Women*, which starred Sophia Loren. I learned later from Rick that he accompanied Ponti to porn theater movie houses to watch porn movies. This was back in the day before the Internet and streaming porn channels up the wazoo. So that was the connection.

We convened at Ross-Gaffney's studio on 46th Street in NYC, a facility we rented occasionally when we needed additional editing space, or a small, inexpensive studio.

Rick, the screen-test shooter, set up five lights, two soft-lights on the background, two floor lights for the actors, and one top-light to highlight the hair and shoulders, especially flattering for the starlets who came to read. The medium and equipment, for anyone who cares, was 16mm reversal film running on an Arri-BL with an Angenieux 12-120 lens; audio was going onto quarter-inch tape on a Nagra recorder with crystal synch.

There was no script. The actors worked in pairs, and were told to improvise a short dramatic scene. This is a tremendous challenge; some of them had never met before, and suddenly they had maybe three minutes to work up a dramatic sketch, and then play it, in one take, in front of Carlo Ponti, for a shot at a real role in a major motion picture with Sophia Loren. I don't know how they do it, but they did, and they were amazingly good.

There was a break in the action in the middle of the day; there were no actors in the hallway ready to test, and Rick had gone to the bathroom. I was chatting with Ponti about New York production. Out of nowhere, he asked me what kind of camera we were using.

"That's an Arri," I said. "It's a German rig, the workhorse of the industry. Designed by two guys, Arnold and Richter, back in the twenties and thirties. Went through World War two, in the trenches. It's almost impossible to break the thing. In '47 it was used to shoot "Dark Passage" with Bogart and Bacall. This one is a 16mm BL, a self-blimped silent camera, for shooting synch sound."

"Uh huh," said Carlo. "And the lens, is that German, too?"

"No, that's French. It's an Angenieux zoom, 12 to 120, which means it has a ten-to-one zoom ratio. It's the top of the line zoom for this format. Smooth, and about as sharp as a zoom can be."

"How about the tape recorder?" asked Carlo.

"That's a Nagra. It's Swiss. No professional audio person uses anything else. Engineered by Kudelski, this audio genius. The Nagra has a crystal-synch motor. Runs at exactly the same speed at the camera, so the picture and sound will synch up later."

"Uh huh," said Carlo.

"This tripod is a Sachtler 7+7, German, and costs about seven grand. The head is an O'Connor 100 fluid head, American."

"Seven thousand, huh," said Carlo, eyeballing the tripod and probably trying to figure out, like the rest of us in the business, what the hell cost seven thousand dollars.

"The shotgun microphone is a Sennheiser, German, and the best of breed. We have some lavalier microphones standing by, in case we decide to mike individual actors. The lavs are made by Sony. Japanese, of course."

"Okay," said Ponti. "So nothing here is Italian?"

I was about to tell Carlo that we had ordered some pizzas for lunch, and they would be Italian, but then I remembered that the pizza place was owned and operated by Greeks.

"Wait a minute," I said. I walked out on the set to check the lights. The stands were Lowells, from America; heads were Mole-Richardsons, also from the states. The bulbs inside them were from Bosch, a German firm. Then I realized, with relief, that the top-light was a Frezzolini. I pointed at the top-light.

"This is Italian," I said. "Frezzolini. Independents love his lights. They're light, flexible, reliable, and easy to set up and break down."

"Good," said Carlo. "At least something on the set other than me is Italian." I laughed because it was funny. Rick came back from the bathroom, a couple of actors showed up to test, and we went back to work.

I spent the rest of the day kicking myself for spending twelve million hours of my life learning all about equipment and how to operate and maintain it, when it was clear that the consummate motion picture producer, Carlo Ponti, didn't know or care if the camera was made from Wisconsin green cheese, and the lens was frozen Jell-O from Afghanistan. Ponti was a producer, he didn't have time to worry about which camera to use, or whose raw stock to buy, or any other technical detail; he trusted his craftsperson, techs and specialists to do their jobs and make those decisions.

CHAPTER 12 STARS GET THERE BY BEING TALENTED

I was taking a meeting, as they say, in my film/video production company office on the 37th floor of the Time & Life Building in Manhattan. Sitting across from me was Sid (fictitious name) a pudgy, well-dressed retired doctor and medical plan administrator. He had heard about me through a friend of a friend. The ex-doctor had heard that I was looking for a project – to make an independent feature film.

"Independent means low budget, right, Ken?" Sid said.

"Right," said I. "Low budget, but not a piece of crap."

"Uh huh."

"I'm a line producer, an actual hands-on producer, not an Executive Producer who brings in money, or who sleeps with the person bringing in the money. I am a producer producer, who has his hand on the helm, controls the major elements, the money, the pre-production, production and post production. I know where and how to save, and where and how to spend."

"So, what are we talking, ballpark, to fund an independent picture?"

"A million, three," I said confidently. "Every dollar is used to raise production values and appear on-screen. I can produce a full-blown picture in digital video, with no big names above the line, but some decent talent, for very close to a million three."

"Now, the person who came up with this million three, he would be the producer, right?"

"Uh huh. 'Executive Producer.'"

"But someone who delivered *all* the money, he would be the *Producer* Producer, right?"

"Generally, yes. But sometimes he might also be a co-producer with another producer. You know, like when one person is putting up the money and the other person is a major element putting up his brand name value, or all the know-how, or his street cred, or marquee value."

"And the Producer, the one putting up *all* the money, he has the power to hire and fire anyone, and to approve or not. To approve the director, screenplay, and casting, right?"

"Well, in practice, the..."

"So, Ken, here's my offer. I give you the million three, and you star my son, the actor, in an independent picture. What do you say?"

"Uh, uh, I say, well, that sounds great, but first I'd like to meet your son and see, you know, if he's..."

"If he's what? He's an actor. You star him in the movie and you've got a movie. If you don't, I take my million three and walk across the street, and find a producer that wants to make a fully funded independent picture starring my son the actor."

"I would love to take your money and invest it in a picture, but what if your boy, for example, isn't compelling on-screen? What if the camera hates him?"

"You'll fix it, Ken. You'll make him look good. You're a smart director, right? They made Peter Fonda look good. And Woody Allen, Schwarzenegger, and, and, that guy with the squinty eyes, Charles Bronson. C'mon, aren't you confident of your skills?"

"Yes, I am, but there has to be some shred of talent, some... has your son ever worked on a feature before?

"Who gives a rat's ass? Have you ever directed a feature before? Jesus, you've never made a feature before, so you couldn't be any good. Is that what you're saying?"

"Behind the camera and in front of it are two very different things."

"Kenny, Kenny, Kenny. Are you in or not?"

"I'd like to meet your son before I make any promises. I think that's only fair, to me, and to you. And to him."

"Fine, fine. Jesus Christ, Cecil B. DeSensitive. Meet my son. I'll tell him to call you, and you'll meet him, and then we'll talk."

"I'll see him as soon as I can, and I'll get right back to you."

"I hope you're such a stickler when you're spending my money." the gargantuan would-be producer struggled to his feet. My admin entered, pulled up alongside him like a zoo attendant sidling up to an elephant, and guided him out of the office.

The son, Avram (name changed to protect whatever) called within the hour and set up an appointment to drop by the next afternoon at 3:30 p.m.

Avram showed up twenty minutes late. My secretary showed him into my office. I looked up from a script and focused my eyes on the most pathetic shred of a quasi-human being I have ever cringed at. The words that popped into my head were "sawed-off homely shrimp."

"Hello, I'm Avram," he lisped, tiny bits of spittle flying off his petulantly poised lower lip. He tentatively offered his hand, which hung from the end of his scrawny wrist like a limp leaf of three-week-old Romaine lettuce that had been peed on by a drunkard with terminal albuminuria. Avram was around eighty pounds, tiny, weak-looking, ugly, pock-marked, wimpy, hirsute, pale as a corpse, and as gay as a chartreuse feather boa twisting through the NOLA French Quarter in a Mardi Gras parade. Not that there's anything wrong with that.

"Avram!" I said, enthusiastically, in a knee-jerk cockeyed attempt to cover my flabbergastedness. I shook his hand as gently as I could and was sure I broke at least two metacarpals anyway. Avram shriveled into the nearest chair; it was like watching a starved and exhausted albino bat fold up for the night. This guy makes Woody Allen look like Charles Atlas, I thought. The only way on earth I could star him in a picture would be to do a comedy.

"So, Avram, how do you feel about comedy?" I asked.

"I don't like it," Avram puled. "It's too hard, and you have to make a fool of yourself to get a laugh. I'm a legitimate actor. I'm excited by drama. I don't want to do comedy."

"Well, frankly, I can't think how else to use you."

"I brought a script I wrote. The Life and Times of Franz Kafka. I would play Kafka."

"But I bet you'd lose," I said, unable to resist a line from vaudeville I learned from my grandmother. "Look, Avram, I don't want to hurt your feelings, or lose your father's money, but I don't care a rat's ass about Kafka, or his life, not to mention his times. I don't want to think about him, or understand his suffering, or make a deep and moving low-budget picture about his stinking, wretched life."

"Well, then, I guess that's that."

"Yes, I suppose it is."

"I'll tell my father," said Avram, rising, with the tone of a middle-school hall-monitor threatening to report me to the vice-principal.

"Yes, you do that," said I, showing Avram the door. "Give him my regards."

* * *

For many actors who get big roles, in spite of the fact that they suck, and people who get dream jobs, factors that have nothing to do with their appropriateness, ability, talent, experience, or skill often come into play. One famous example, the blonde singer in "Citizen Kane", obviously fashioned after

Marion Davies, the minimally gifted singer, actress and mistress promoted relentlessly by William Randolph Hearst.

Now you know the answer to your question when you see a film, or show, and ask your companion, "How did that piece of crap get *made?*" Or, "How the hell did *she* get that role?" Or, "What the hell is *he* doing starring?" And don't think for a moment that this kind of horsefrocky is restricted to show business. The same kind of scenario plays out every hour of every day in every career everywhere. People who have absolutely no right to do so get the job. People who don't deserve the break get it. It makes no sense at all for so-and-so to get the account, client, assignment, promotion, or raise, but they do.

CHAPTER 13 WHAT YOU NEED IS A BUSINESS PARTNER

I was operating a small ad agency in Fairfield County, Connecticut. The company was me, one designer and one assistant. Since I was the only one out hustling up new business, and could only do one thing at a time, it was a roller coaster ride of busy/not busy. We were either working on a job with a scary deadline, or I was out in the marketplace, selling. In my spare time, I would whine to my staff that if I had a partner, all our problems would be solved. My ideal partner would not duplicate me, but would be strong in areas in which I was not so strong, like management, organization, administration.

"Oh, I know someone, says my designer. He's a one-man company doing mostly collateral print stuff for Archaic & Stodgy Co., and Sleeping Sloth, Inc. (fabricated names of course, along with the one that follows.) His name is Peter Picayune. Do you want me to set up a meeting?"

I met Peter and he seemed just right. He was polite, tall, well-spoken, cordial, smart, conceited and anal. I thought he would make a great administrative type. He had operated an agency with several employees in upstate somewhere, and was doing fine when he got the Hollywood bug, and had just returned from blowing off ten years of his life trying to make it as a writer or producer or director or any damn thing at all that Hollywood would let him do. I could sympathize with some of his background, and empathize with his missteps. He liked the idea of a partnership, too; he had been having the same problems as I with the work-sell cycle. He was doing fairly regular collateral work for Archaic & Stodgy, and said he had done some stuff for Sleeping Sloth, and I had no reason to disbelieve him. I told him I had regular work from a major regional developer, a national printing firm, and an international beverage company, let's call them Big Beverages. It looked like a good match.

We, each put in a thousand dollars, formed an S-Corporation and issued ourselves 500 shares of stock each. I was the president, because I had been the main driver of forming the company, was a couple of years older, the company office was going to be in my house initially, and a lawyer friend of mine was going to set us up for a song. Also, Peter didn't seem to have any current work in house when we formed the new company. He had been out selling, he said.

Christmas rolled around soon after, and my wife and I had Peter and his lady friend over for Christmas dinner. The lady had come up from Washington, DC. I got the feeling that she was hoping for Peter to pop the Big Question, but I got the feeling that he had no intention of doing so anytime in the near future. Everything was lovely, except my wife didn't like Peter. She kept asking him hard questions, like, "Do you have any money to put into this company if Ken's accounts stop ordering stuff for a while?" And, "When are you going to bring some of your accounts into the business?" Peter would glare at her, like, how dare you question me, Peter The Great? I thought my wife was being overly cautious, and moved quickly to smooth things over.

The new company plugged along, doing okay, with my clients: the regional developer, and the national printer, and nothing from Peter. But it became clear soon enough that Peter was definitely doing stuff on the side for the Archaic & Stodgy Company. We talked about it and he said he didn't bring it into our new company because it was old business – something he had initiated before we became partners. And it was only this one thing, and blah, blah, blah. Well, I didn't want to be a penis and destroy our budding partnership with the first little incident, so I went along with his excuse, and he kept his Archaic & Stodgy account in his own pocket.

I had done some small projects for the Big Beverage Company, and an opportunity came up for a bigger job. Peter insisted on being in on the meetings with my client, because if he was a partner, he wanted to be involved in every important phase of servicing the client. Fine, whatever. My contact at Big Beverage was Lucy, a lady in her early thirties who had been dating a guy for some eight years who had walked recently when she gave him a long-overdue ultimatum. I tell you this not because that's what defined Lucy more than her brains or character or talent at corporate politics, but because it's what ended up being a catalyst behind the scenes in the next couple of moves.

I took Peter into the Big Beverage meeting with Lucy, who is attractive and was now available, and Peter is eating her up with his baby blues, and hanging on her every word, and sending her enough signals to jam all the regular broadcasts from the top of the Empire State Building. What about his love-interest from Washington, you ask? Hey, the hell with her – this is business, boys and girls.

So, okay, this isn't necessarily bad, I'm thinking. I like Lucy, and I had been flirting with her myself, although in a harmless, low-key, socially acceptable way. I was a totally married guy; she knew I wasn't going to run away with her for a wild weekend in Rio, and propose on a fine white-sand beach under the moonlight. But Peter was a different story. He was single, tall, and had a dashing beard, which neatly covered his weak chin. He just might run away with her to Rio, or some other romantic place, and take away all the pain of the eight years wasted on the bum that wouldn't commit.

Peter was my partner, and if Lucy fell for his lothario act, that was just fine. If she threw us a couple of big pieces of business, for whatever reason, we would be boarding the gravy train. Meanwhile, I was working on bringing in a new account that wasn't as big as Big Beverage, but it would have been easy to service, and it was local. The guy we had to impress wanted to see us at the end of next week, on a Friday. I called Peter and told him about the meeting, and asked him to go into the presentation with me. He was sorry he couldn't make it – his mother was going into the hospital in New York City for an operation, and he had to be there for her. Well, of course, that was the priority. I called the prospect back and asked if we couldn't move the meeting to the following Monday. No, he was leaving for a trip to the regional sales offices, and wouldn't be back for three weeks. It had to be Friday.

I went into the Friday meeting alone, and did a presentation. Later that evening I got a call from a photographer I knew, a guy whose studio is a couple of towns east of me in Fairfield County.

"Hey," he says, "I shot a session today for this guy, Peter Picayune. I thought he was your partner."

"He is," says I.

"Ken, I gotta tell you, this guy comes in here as an art director, but believe me, he's no art director."

"Right. He *wants* to be an art director someday. He thinks it looks like fun."

"It was a joke. He didn't even have any roughs of what he wanted me to shoot. I asked him questions, and half the time he didn't know what I was talking about. I just thought you should know."

"He told me he had to go into the city because of his poor little old mother's operation. But I know he's doing some brochure for Archaic & Stodgy. Some partner, huh?"

"This wasn't for Archaic & Stodgy. This was for Big Beverage."

"Get outta town."

"Right. A whole new direction for them. Entire new product line. New flavors, new packaging, everything. I'm shooting more stuff next week."

"Please tell me you're kidding."

"This guy was very tight with Lucy. You should have heard him on the phone with her. Sounds like he's like dating her, dude. And for her to send him to art direct a gig like this, he must have her totally snockered."

I tried to phone Peter, and he wasn't in, or wasn't answering. I called my lawyer friend who set up the corporation and told her what had happened.

"Oh, God, that's a shame," she said. "What do you want to do?"

"Kill him," I said.

"No, I mean really."

"No, I mean I really want to kill him. He deserves to be killed. That's why I'm calling you. I figured you'd have a more practical solution."

"Dissolve the corporation and break with the man, ASAP."

"Good. Let's do it."

"All right. I'll set up a meeting early next week. Bring your books, your documents of incorporation, and your checkbook."

"No. Not next week. I want to do it now."

"Ken, it's Friday evening. We can't do it now."

"Tomorrow, then."

"Tomorrow is Saturday."

"So?"

"You're coming from anger now. Let me talk to Peter and then I'll get back to you and we'll try to do this with the least amount of pain."

"Where's Dr. Kevorkian when you need him?"

"Does Peter know that you know, I mean about him going behind your back."

"No."

"Well, stay away from him entirely. Let me do the talking."

"Uh huh."

"Will he be surprised that you want to break up so suddenly?"

"No. We're not having fun. We talked last week about how it wasn't all coming up roses. I thought I was getting a businessman, and instead I get a would-be creative with no ideas."

"Well, I'll track him down. You just calm down and sit tight."

"I'll be sitting by the phone."

"I'll call you back as soon as I've hung up with him."

An hour later she called me back.

"Sheesh, that's the sleaziest snake I ever talked with," she said. "Under which rock did you find this guy?"

"So, now what?"

"You could sue for embezzlement, and fraud, and a couple of other things. But it would probably involve your client at Big Beverage, and you said she's romantically involved with him, so you'd end up losing that business for sure."

"How much would it cost to sue? And is there any way I could lose?"

"It would cost a bunch, and take time as well. And you would probably win, but that's not the point. You want my advice, here's my advice. If you sue him, you're going to have to be involved with him for a long time, maybe years. He'll countersue on some trumped up garbage. Your ex-client lady may be in love with the guy, in which case you don't know what she'd say in court. You could lose the business, and the case, too. Then there's all the time to fight the case. Plus all the money. And he'll be in your face, and your mind, the whole time. You'll never get a decent night's sleep. And you might just lose it somewhere along the way and kill the sleazebag after all. My advice to you is to break all ties to this man as soon and as thoroughly as possible. You'll have to split with him whatever's in the account right now, minus your accounts payable, but plus your accounts receivable."

"I have to pay this peckerhead for screwing me?"

"Yes, and well worth it. You give him half the money, he resigns as an officer and a director, returns the stock and that's that."

"All right."

"I've set it up for tomorrow at 11:00 am. I pushed for my office, but he insisted it had to be at his house."

"He thinks that'll prevent me from ripping off his head and hurling it out the window."

"There'll be no hurling of heads. I want your word."

"I'll try my best."

"You sound very... angry. Maybe we should put it off for a couple of days."

"No, let's do it tomorrow. I'll be perfectly civilized."

"I'll have to testify against you if you kill him. Just so you know."

"The law is an ass."

When I got to Peter Picayune's despicable cottage the next morning, he and my lawyer lady were sitting at the dining room table passing papers back and forth. The only place for me to sit was across the table from Peter. It was a wide table. This was strategy: it would make it hard for me reach across and rip out his split-tongued double-talking throat. I made a mental note that it was a heavy oak table, and my first move if I went postal would be to flip the table over into his lap, pinning him into his chair, and holding him in place while I yanked his head clean off his sallow, epicene neck. He was taller than me by about two to three inches, but I had not a moment's doubt that I would destroy him in a matter of seconds. I also noticed that he had put out of sight anything that I could use as a weapon.

My lawyer conducted the meeting, in which I was required to write Peter a check for half the money in our account. I couldn't help pointing out, with righteous indignation, that not one penny of that money had come from one of Peter's accounts. And as far as his contribution to the work I did, I reminded him of the fact that he did nothing.

"It's just business," he said. Yes, he actually said that, folks. He had no idea at that moment how close he came to experiencing the forcible removal of his larynx by bare enraged hands. The lawyer immediately jumped in with the next piece of business, which was the issue of the non-compete clause in Peter's resignation document. This was great fun, because he didn't know that the lawyer lady and I both knew that he had gone behind my back with my Big Beverage account. If he signed the document with the non-compete clause intact, he was dead in the water.

"I think that's... inappropriate," he said to the lawyer. The clause stipulated that Peter would not go after one of my accounts for a period of three years.

"It certainly is appropriate," she replied. "Why do you think it's part of the boilerplate language of every executive employment contract?"

"I don't care about boilerplate," the rodent said. "I'm just not going to sign such a thing. My attorney advised me not to sign any non-compete clause."

"Would you prefer me to shorten the term, say, to one year?" asked my attorney.

"I will not sign any non-compete clause, of any term, on the advice of my attorney, and that's that," Peter replied, his pallid color darkening with the bile of guilt pumping through his traitorous veins. I think by now he must have suspected that I had somehow found out about his end-run with Big Beverage.

The lawyer lady ran her pen through the clause and passed it to me to initial, and then to Peter for him to initial. She figured we'd had enough fun with the deceitful penis, and now it was time to move on and get this nasty business wrapped up. So we tallied the numbers in the company account and divided the total by two, and I was writing Peter a check when he said he wouldn't accept a check from me.

He was worried, lads and lassies, that I would stop payment on the check. Suddenly we were deadlocked. There was talk of meeting at the bank on Monday to deposit the check to Peter's account, and when the officer told him it cleared, Peter would sign his resignation and turn over his stock. But I didn't want to wait till Monday, and I didn't want to ever have to see Peter's lying face again. The lawyer lady saved the day:

"No problem: I'll write you a check on my trust account, and I'll take the business check from Ken," she suggested.

"How do I know you won't stop payment on your check?" asks the sleaze-ball of my attorney. This lawyer lady has such a sterling reputation in the community that I would trust her with my life and everything I own. I never met a more scrupulous person in my life. I saw her cheeks burn at the suggestion that she would do something illegal or out of line. But she sucked it up and answered his pathetic innuendo calmly and professionally.

"I have an attorney's fiduciary responsibility to pass through funds as required by law. If I stopped payment or in any way impeded your collection, I could be disbarred, get a huge fine, and go to jail. It would not be worth it, I assure you."

That seemed to satisfy the sniveling roach. He accepted the lawyer's check, folded it and put it in his pocket, then signed the necessary documents. No one shook hands. Peter sensed that if he extended his arm out, I would have yanked it clean out of its socket and used it to beat him senseless. I just got up and walked out.

The lawyer and I shook hands outside on the street. "Expensive lesson," she said, handing me the documents.

"Uh huh," said I, still precipitously on the edge of my rage.

"He thinks he won," she said. "But, believe me, you won. You got rid of him fast and clean, and you didn't have to decapitate him and hurl his head out the window. Count your blessings."

"Yes, I suppose. Thank you for mediating, and for coming with such short notice on a Saturday."

"I thought it was worth keeping a client from the electric chair, or a life in prison."

"Then again, killing him would have had a certain sacramental purity to it."

"You know, I suppose so."

CHAPTER 14 DO THIS JOB CHEAP, AND GET A BIG JOB LATER

It took me five years of storming the citadel to get some business from Pitney Bowes, the postage meter and office document people once headquartered in a massive "Mother Ship" in Stamford, CT. Pitney Bowes was, at the apogee of their success curve, one very obstinate nut to crack. They were romanced by every supplier and vendor on earth, so they had developed a frosty, hard-to-get attitude. And I was selling industrial film and video services, along with eighty nine million other supplicants, so it was a really hard connection to make.

But anyway, through tenacity, patience, good timing, good luck, and long life, I finally got some business from the sacred halls of Pitney Bowes. I produced a number of sales films for them, things they used as sales tools, for salespeople and at trade shows. And the last couple I did I produced for a golden–haired new, young efficiency expert who was all over my budgets, and joyfully sucked out all the cushions I had built in to every major facet of production.

In other words, I ended up making the last couple of programs for nickels and dimes. But he encouraged me to hang in, because, he assured me, there were some really important projects coming up, and I would be given preferential treatment in bidding on those big budget projects.

But then the wheel of fortune turned, and Pitney Bowes' golden-haired, new, young exec, on the crest of his corporate wave, was suddenly shanghaied away by British Airways! At his new job in their broadcast advertising department, he was contracting for Heavy Duty, Big Budget TV spots. I couldn't believe my luck; a guy that I was tight with, for whom I had done great work, was now in a position to award me some international Class-A jobs!

But, curb your enthusiasm folks -- he didn't call back, and he wouldn't even take my calls, in NYC or London. I finally got through to him by saying I was his dentist, I asked him what the story was.

"I'm sorry, Ken," he said, "you have to understand, this is really Class-A, top-of-the-line stuff I'm doing now."

"I can do that. You know how creative I am. I want a shot at producing your Class-A, top-of-the-line stuff. How about you at least let me bid on a couple of things?"

"Frankly, Ken, there's really no point. It's not a budget thing, you know. I mean, budget is not an issue. I'm working with stars now, Ridley Scott, and Becker. I just took a meeting with Michael Cimino."

"But, but..."

"The people I'm working with now never heard of you, Ken. Sorry, old buddy, but it's out of the question."

"Right. How silly of me. I don't know what I was thinking."

"Tootle-do."

"Yes, tootle-do it is."

CHAPTER 15   NEVER GIVE UP ON YOUR DREAM

It was 1980, and I was a guest in a lush, high-ceilinged, beautifully decorated and furnished apartment in New York's east Sixties attending an angels' reading of my brilliantly funny play, *Next to Closing*. Jed Feuer, the son of Cy Feuer of Feuer and Martin fame ("Guys and Dolls," "Cabaret," "How to Succeed in Business Without Really Trying," etc.) was going to produce my play. Jed had been working with me for many months, fine-diddling the thing one way or another to make it just perfect. Cy had read the final script and he told me I was "the funniest guy in the East, as long as Doc Simon stayed on the Coast." My "Next to Closing" was a funny script. Very very funny.

The wealthy investor who owned the apartment wasn't there. His wife was, initially, but she had to go somewhere and couldn't stay for the reading. We had the use of the apartment for the reading, and six or seven uber-rich angels that Jed had invited. An angel is a theatrical investor, and an angels', or backers' reading is a non-staged reading of a new work by the best actors you can get for the occasion, with the intention of convincing the angels to cough up the angel-dust needed to produce the play.

I was operating a film and video production company in Manhattan at that time, so I knew plenty of good casting agents and actors. Jed knew a couple more. Everyone who saw the script had high hopes for this play, so we got some terrific actors to read for the angels. I have lost all the documentation from this august event, so I can't give you the names of the actors, sorry. Except, of course, my father, Kenny "Senator Claghorn" Delmar, the former luminary of the golden age of radio.

The eight actors, Jed and I arrived a half an hour before the angels. We got the actors arranged how we wanted them at one end of the vast living room. They all had received the script a week earlier, and didn't need much direction. We read pieces of a few scenes and it sounded great, sounded like the angels couldn't fail to be dazzled by the staggering brilliance of the piece, if not first knocked senseless by its singular humor.

The angels showed up one at a time, as if each one didn't want to have to ride the elevator with the other. Some men, some women, all of them oozing multi-millions from every pore. One of them, I recall, was a world-class beauty, the young American wife of a Greek shipping tycoon. No, not Jackie. Better. Younger, and more beautiful.

Bowing and scraping, cheerful smiles on our faces, Jed and I unctuously steered the angels to seats at the other side of the capacious living room. When everyone was comfortable, Jed welcomed the angels and enthused about the play. I set the scene, and we launched into the reading proper.

About halfway through page one, a little white dog danced into the middle of the marble vestibule that adjoined the living room and began to bark. I think it was a poodle, but it might have been one of those arcane off-breeds related to the poodle, but including, in its DNA chain, bits of chromosomes from wolves, whooping cranes, and actual Frenchmen. The dog was a rabid Type-A killer that would never forgive the world for having shrunken him down to a size that prevented him from reaching the jugular veins of annoying upright adult humans.

Fido's nervous bark was not a steady chain of yips, but a broken one, in which he would bark a few times, then listen to hear if our ear bones were still rattling, or how much he had aggravated us. But beyond the thought-shattering horror of the bark itself, this mad dog somehow knew just *when* to bark. Whenever there was a punchline, he would bark. Right on it, obliterating it completely. How could he do that?

Jed went into the vestibule, since I was busy reading the stage directions, and tried to get rid of the dog by herding it into another room. This produced a cacophony of noise so jarring and bloodcurdling that the actors and I had to stop reading. We sipped water and made small talk with the angels, who tried to look as understanding as rich people can under such stressful circumstances. A few minutes later, Jed, having had a short discussion with the live-in housekeeper, who spoke no English, came in and announced that it wouldn't be possible to lock the dog out of the living room because it made him feel insecure and his analyst forbade it. You can't make stuff like this up, boys and girls.

In any case, the proposed solution, conveyed via gesticulation and homemade semaphore signals by the housekeeper, was that we were all to move to the huge dining room, which we all did, with the actors moving to one side of a long, massive wooden table, and the angels to the other. We continued the reading where we had left off, in the middle of page two.

We got up to speed again, and were galloping along nicely when an earthquake hit. Well, it felt like an earthquake, with vibrations coming through the floor strong enough to induce orgasms in the elderly. But it sounded worse than any earthquake; it sounded like blithering Armageddon. It sounded like twelve angry war-apes in the apartment below were fighting it out with fifty millimeter machine guns. I'm not kidding. Sometimes I have been known to exaggerate, but I swear, I'm not exaggerating. It took a little while to figure out the noise was coming from below, because it was so loud you couldn't tell where it was coming from. Actors and angels looked worried. Like some *force majeure* was happening, something really massive and terminal, like Judgement Day. Most of the actors didn't look like they wanted their careers to end quite yet. And the angels didn't look like they were ready to be judged yet. What to do, what to do? The little white dog got out of wherever the housekeeper had put him, ran beneath our feet and started barking as hard as he could, and you couldn't hear him at all. Served him right.

Time to act, I resolved, with my last cogent semblance of a thought. I rang for the elevator and took it down one flight to the floor below, where the sound appeared to be mainly coming from. The elevator door opened and I saw, there and into the foyer of the adjoining apartment, a cloud of plaster and concrete dust, a half a dozen construction guys from Con Edison, and a New York cop. Heavy cables or air hoses snaked in from the front of the building. Two of the guys were operating industrial-size jackhammers.

Yes, folks, pneumatic jackhammers, like you see in the streets of the city, breaking up the macadam. The other guys had on those big plastic earphones that look like humpback turtles trying to crush human heads between them. The cop was holding his hands over his ears. The guys with the jackhammers were at work on a stout plaster or stucco chase at the edge of the vestibule. I screamed at them to stop, but, of course, no one heard me. I waded into the sea of sweat, dust, biceps and tattoos and yanked on guys' arms to get their attention. Finally, the two guys with the jackhammers shut them off and looked at me. The cop was already wrapping his fingers around my arm.

"What the fuck?" cried one of the hammer operators, pulling one side of his earphones to reveal a piece of angry cauliflower ear.

"You gotta STOP!" I cried. "We're reading my play upstairs for a group of angels, you know, rich people who will pay for the production. They can't hear a thing! You have to stop!"

"No way, pal. Water's leaking here on a power main. Could go any minute. Take down the whole building, maybe the street...the whole grid."

"How about you give me one hour of quiet and I give you a hundred bucks?" I said, reaching for my wallet.

"Fuggedaboudit," said one of the hammer operators. "No can do." They re-donned their earphones, turned their jackhammers back on and continued to attack the column of plaster shrouding the leaking pipe. I grabbed for an arm, and upped my offer to two hundred dollars, but then I was either blown back by the noise, or yanked back by the strong arms of construction guys and the cop. And then they were passing me to the back of the huddle, out of the way, like an ugly, fat guy when he tries to body-surf the mosh pit. Finally, just before my eardrums turned into tapioca pudding and my head exploded like a ripe melon, I broke away and rang for the elevator. It didn't come for a long time. Something about the power being turned off while the workers were near the line. When I finally got back upstairs, Jed and the housekeeper and the manic dog were all that remained. The actors had left, the angels had left...they had taken the service stairs in the back, all glad to be out of there with their lives and their eardrums intact.

Fifteen minutes later I was walking alone south on Park Avenue toward Grand Central Station. I knew that was it, the death of the play. Jed had tried to reassure me that it wasn't the end of the world, but I knew it was the final straw in a chain of bad breaks that made it look like The Fates had singled me out for termination with prejudice. *Next to Closing* was not destined to be done, no matter what we did, and that was that.

* * *

Most people have to give up on The Big Dream and settle for the smaller, more reasonable dream, or no dream at all, because of one damn thing or another. It's just not in the cards. Things don't work out. The discipline they chose withers away. The company they chose has a change of fortune. The region they chose loses momentum. The market dies or moves away. They are hit by a pick-up truck driven by an alien with no insurance. A trend becomes and un-trend. The star they hitched their wagon to sputtered and fell from the firmament.

"Next To Closing" was never produced. Cy Feuer died. Sid Caesar, who was supposed to star, died. And Jed Feuer, who was set to produce, became a trumpet player and formed a band in New York City. Every few years I send him an email. He's okay.

CHAPTER 16
BUSINESSPEOPLE ARE
BASICALLY HONEST

H ere's a story that is perhaps typical of the big
city, one that I will try my best to tell
objectively, which will be a challenge because I
got to play the role of trusting gullible sap.

A couple of years after I started my film production
company in NYC, I leased some space next to Mathison-Ress,
an advertising agency that did not have a TV department, or
anyone on staff with TV writing or production experience. I
had a connection to the agency in that my dad was friends with
the President and founder, Irwin Ress, an ex-group head from
a large, older agency. Irwin had secured an introduction to a
Rick Appleman of Faberge (Now a part of Unilever), which then
led to meeting George Barrie, the president and CEO of
Faberge. Irwin learned that Barrie had returned recently from
Japan, where he had become fascinated with a stunning shade

of yellow taken from the Japanese chrysanthemum, and he was working on a new line of products for the bath packaged in this brilliant yellow. Barrie wanted a dazzling creative TV campaign that would help sell the new line, Kiku. Irwin asked if Mathison–Ress could take a shot at making a proposal, and Barrie said okay.

Irwin called me in when he returned to his office, and explained the opportunity. Since I was a TV producer/director, but had come from copywriting, he threw the creative challenge in my lap, and wanted to see something as soon as possible. I came back the next morning with a campaign based on the sun, and sunlight, sprinkled with images of things that were bright yellow, like a sunrise, canary, gold, blonde hair, etc. I wrote two thirty second spots that came at this theme from different angles. Since I can draw, and Ress didn't have a storyboard artist on staff, I drew the boards myself that night.

The next day Irwin looked at the spots and loved them. He also liked the way I presented them, and invited me to come with him into George Barrie's handsome brownstone quite close to the Museum of Modern Art in Manhattan.

I presented the two storyboards to Barrie. He chose the one he liked the best, which featured a bright yellow sunrise and a beautiful blonde running on a beach, and told us to go ahead and produce it. Money was not discussed in this meeting, although Barrie asked about costs, because Irwin muttered some bullshit about not having had time to cost out the spots. But, he said, if Barrie wanted us to produce one or more, Irwin would get right back to him with the numbers. The truth was that I had completed thorough budgets for the spots, but Irwin told me we shouldn't present those at the same time as creative, as a matter of form. I didn't think about it at the time, but somewhere in here it dawned on me that Irwin's real agenda was that he was going to mark the spots up, way past my conservative budgets, and he didn't want me to hear the number and give it away by howling "Are you shittin' me?!"

The budget I had given Irwin indicated that I could produce the spot in 16mm for twenty five thousand dollars. This was a bargain basement budget for a national spot, with two on-camera SAG actors, a voice-over, several locations, and a fancy, revolving product shot – but I was young and hungry, I had never worked for a TV spot production company, so what did I know? At the $25,000 figure, I would be making about $6,000 profit, and I figured that was fair. Yes, boys and girls, I came up with a budget and profit target that was fair – go ahead and have a hearty laugh at my naïve expense. The only positive light you could shine on my ridiculously low estimate was that I figured it would surely land me future production work from Mathison-Ress.

I subsequently learned that Irwin didn't mark the spot up the standard 17.65%, or even a whopping 50%, which isn't unheard of, but marked it up a rapacious 200%. Such an egregious markup was only possible because I was holding costs down by doing so much of the work myself (writing, boarding, presenting casting, location scouting, shooting, directing, editing, mixing). The money I would be saving Irwin by knocking myself out would go into Irwin's pocket. Hey, that makes sense. At least, if you look on the bright side, I would end up with a national spot for a household-name client on my reel, and that's a bankable benefit.

When Irwin came to my office to give me the go-ahead, he brought with him the letter of agreement I had drafted, and a check for one thousand dollars.

"What's this for?" I asked.

"Oh, just earnest money," Irwin said, with a smile. "For presenting to the client, for going above and beyond the call, and moving so quickly."

"Thanks," I said, taking the check. "This is in addition to the budget, right?"

"Yes, of course," he said, smiling again and putting his hand on my shoulder. "Just do a great job, and we'll all make money."

So that's what I did. I produced the spot, with Rick Appleman coming in at crucial points to approve. George Barrie and Rick loved the finished spot, and it went straight to air nationally. Initially it was going to run thirteen weeks, but it did so well, they ran it for fifty two weeks. The models, the couple I had hired as non-speaking principals made enough money from the spot that they sold their home in Montclair, NJ, and moved to Hollywood. And the voice-over guy couldn't believe the residuals that kept pouring in.

But, guess what, fellow scouts? *I never saw another penny.* Thirty days passed, then forty five, then sixty, then ninety. I took the bookkeeper to lunch, and found out from her that Faberge had paid for the spot long ago, and was throwing lots more money into air-time. So, why wasn't I being paid for the creative and production? The bookkeeper didn't know; she had submitted my invoice for approval several times, but it just never came back with an approval. There were priorities, she suggested, like payroll, and rent. First things first. I tried to explain to her that paying me was just as important as payroll and rent, because without me, there would be no commercial, and no big media dollars coming in to implement it. She ducked by saying it wasn't her decision, and I should keep nagging Irwin.

So I kept nagging Irwin. Six or seven more weeks passed, and finally I hired a lawyer-friend to nag Irwin. It was getting close to Christmas, and I could certainly have used the money that was due me. Also, I had paid for the entire production out of my pocket, including the union crew, staff, rawstock, SAG actors, the lab, the optical house, equipment rental, studio, transfers to videotape, post-house, audio recording and mixing etc. My lawyer, Jack Scherer, a friend who had graduated from Middlebury a year ahead of me, called me and told me he had done well: he had secured from Irwin a stack of post-dated checks, twenty four of them, for one thousand dollars each, one per month, starting a month hence.

"Thanks," I said, "but have come to believe that a post-dated check from Irwin isn't worth diddly." I guess Jack hadn't been in practice long enough to know how deceitful people in the Big Apple can be.

"But, Ken, he *likes* you," said Jack. "He wants to do more spots with you."

"Right," said I, "How much do you want to bet that not one of these checks clears – ever?"

"He wouldn't dare do that," said Jack. "It's a federal offence."

"Are they gonna come and arrest him and throw him in jail?"

"Maybe not, but they can garnish his salary, and..."

"So, he'll stop paying himself. He'll pay more to his wife (his executive VP). He's never going to pay me. I'm not a priority. I really should just kill the guy."

"Jeez, Ken, you gotta have a little faith. He told me they have another big investor ready to pump in a bunch of capital into the company. You just gotta hang in a little longer. He's gonna need more spots, and then he's going to have to pay you for the last one first."

Christmas came and went. The twenty seven employees of Mathison-Ress came back from their Christmas holiday, and lo and behold – *all their paychecks had bounced*! Irwin, who usually came in early, was nowhere to be seen. The receptionist and a few other employees started to make calls to find him, but in vain. The scary thing was that Irwin's office had been emptied of all his personal stuff; his prized eight-foot marlin, mounted on the wall behind his desk, was gone. That was a bad sign. His wife's office, and their personal secretary's desk were thoroughly cleared out as well. All three of them were gone, vanished like assistants in a David Copperfield illusion. The funny thing was that it took a while for us to get our heads around the fact that Irwin, his wife and their admin had absconded. A few employees were still on the phone trying to contact one of the three miscreants, thinking that it was either a joke or a mistake, or maybe they were just setting up a new office somewhere, and they would call us at any minute to cover our bounced checks and pay us severance or ask us if we wanted to join them in the new office, wherever it might be. Hope springs eternal.

Around mid-day, and through the afternoon creditors, marshals and repo men began to show up at the office. Everything in the place, it turned out, was leased, right down to and including the carpeting. Sheriffs and marshals and various repossessors were taking out everything they could carry, and tagging everything they would come back to get later. Employees sat at their desks, out of habit, in shock, wondering how they were going to cover their Christmas purchases. And suddenly the desk would be moving up and away, into the firm grips of burly moving men. Within three days the office was a shell of its former self. I had to move, of course, as I had been subletting from Irwin. The landlord was not a happy camper; Irwin had been behind in his rent.

Larry Lowenstein, Irwin's partner, was in his largely empty office, filling a cardboard box with some of the items the marshals and repo men hadn't packed out of the space. Larry, although a partner, had not been in on the ugly exit play, and was as much in shock as the rest of us.

Larry had an interesting bit of information to pass on: A wealthy investor who lived in New Jersey had had a long-time crush on Irwin's wife, Nancy, who was beautiful and bright. Instead of throwing a jealousy fit, like a normal husband would, Irwin sort of looked the other way, and let the smitten investor pine away for his wife. There was an agenda here: the investor had been keeping Nancy and Irwin in his life by promising to make an investment in the firm. Irwin had been stalling us all until the check from this guy cleared. As I recall, Larry said he'd heard the investment was in the neighborhood of $185,000, a handsome premium in the early seventies. Whatever the amount, the minute the check cleared, the proceeds were wired to a second corporation in California, and Irwin et al flew the coop. With him went the wife/exec VP, and the large personal secretary that the two of them shared.

Irwin and his wife had cleaned out the Mathison-Ress accounts of every penny, and "invested" it, plus the money the angel in New Jersey had just put in, in *another* corporation that had been set up in California. That's legal in US corporate law, you see. As the CEO of company A, a corporation in which he and his wife held the majority stock, Irwin could decide to invest Corporation A's cash into Corporation B, of which the two of them happened to hold all the stock. In this way, it's legal to plunder your own company and screw everyone in it, but keep your own financial ass intact. Welcome to American-style capitalism, folks.

There were no clues, as to where Irwin, Nancy, and their secretary had gone. For all practical purposes, Scotty had beamed them up. Within a couple of weeks, there were some thirty-one warrants for Irwin in New York City, from a parade of angry creditors. But they would all have to bite the bullet – there was no Irwin or Nancy to serve.

Just as I warned my attorney, the pile of thousand dollar checks he had extracted from Irwin were not worth the paper upon which they were written. There was no point trying to get money from Faberge; they had already paid the agency for the spot, plus all the money they had thrown into running the hell out of it on air.

Jack explained my options: I should go bankrupt; that was the sensible thing to do. I didn't like the sound of the word bankrupt – I had only been in business for two years; it didn't seem like an auspicious beginning. So I asked my creditors, one by one, for their patience and understanding while I paid them over time. They all said they understood, and that they would hang in there. They didn't have much choice, really; bankruptcy would have left them with nothing, or pennies on the dollar. I made the last payment due five years later, to Movielab, the New York film lab.

Irwin was apprehended some months after his Christmas caper at Los Angeles airport, I heard from a fellow burned creditor, getting on a plane with Nancy for Vancouver, Canada (and from there, God knows where?). Irwin was caught not by one of the detectives, private eyes, agents, lawyers or marshals looking for him on both coasts, but by one of his ex-wives lawyers. We were glad of the news, but it didn't mean much to most of us he owed money to in New York, since we had been shafted in a legal fashion, and Irwin was protected by his corporate machinations. Of course, his attorneys had him out five minutes after they brought him in (for lack of child support, or alimony, I understood), and he dropped from view again immediately.

There is a fantastic postscript to this story, you can call it karma, or retribution, or just desserts, or whatever you like:

Some years after the fly-by-night departure, Irwin reappeared in a short and shocking way. It was his birthday, I don't know which one, maybe his forty seventh. He and his wife, Nancy, were staying in their Manhattan condo on the seventeenth floor. I remember the seventeenth floor because it was also the seventeenth of September. It was early in the morning, and I was standing in front of the sink shaving. A radio announcer on one of the morning news programs was reading the latest items. This isn't verbatim, but captures the gist:

"Last night wealthy advertising executive, Irwin Ress, plunged to his death from the seventeenth story Manhattan condo owned by him and his wife. Police on the scene reported that his wife said that Ress had committed suicide."

There may have been some other information, like the exact time of the incident, or the fact that Nancy, was with him just before he jumped, but I don't remember hearing or understanding anything else. I was so struck by the impact of the news that I ran down to the kitchen to tell my wife about it. After I finished my morning ablutions, I spent about an hour on the phone, talking to people close to the Mathison-Ress misadventure. It may have been during these calls, or a few days or weeks later that I learned, from someone close to Nancy who talked to her about it, what happened the night Irwin went to the Big Agency in The Sky. You appreciate that this is hearsay two sets of ears removed, but there would be no point in lying, so I have accepted it as a fairly accurate account of what happened, and will pass it on to you with that caveat.

It was Irwin's birthday, but Nancy couldn't call anyone to come over for a party, because no one could know they were in New York City. There were plenty of warrants still in effect.

Plus there were a lot of people, like myself, one jump ahead of bankruptcy, who would have liked to run into Irwin and give him a good, hard punch in the nose, followed by knocking him down and kicking in a few of his ribs. But I digress.

They were out on their seventeenth-floor balcony, overlooking the city. Nancy went back inside to get a bottle of champagne. When she returned, Irwin had disappeared. He couldn't have gotten past her without her seeing him... then she saw eight white knuckles wrapped across the top edge of the stone parapet. She rushed to the parapet. It was Irwin, of course, hanging on for dear life. He looked up at Nancy, one can only imagine his expression. She grabbed onto his wrists and tried to help him up. But Irwin was not athletic, and on the plump side, and Nancy was petite, and had a congenital issue with one shoulder. There was no way they were going to get him back up and over the parapet. Irwin's life was going to come to an abrupt end within the next several seconds.

"Oh my God!" Nancy cried. "What happened?"

"Everyone said I deserved to die," gasped Irwin. "So I stood on the edge and said, 'God, what do you say?' Then came this gust of wind." Nancy looked away as Irwin's fingers slipped out of hers.

CHAPTER 17   HOW TO MOVE DISTRESSED MERCHANDISE

Media Bartering Services (not their real name. I have changed the name because a few of the players are still around, and a cousin of mine was married to the CEO) was one of the earliest and biggest corporate barter companies to appear in the '70s and flourish for 15+ years. My connection, other than the family one mentioned above, was that I produced a few TV spots for them. MBS was founded by a man who operated a company that created and aired TV spots for products that were not available in stores, but only through special TV offers. This man, let's call him Jack, had to maintain a low profile because he was being pitilessly pursued by attorneys representing his four ex-wives, so when he founded Media Bartering

Services, he asked a colleague, let's call him Orca, to take the role of CEO and sit in the big corner office.

Media Bartering Services (MBS) had a very compelling business model. They would contact a manufacturer, or importer of products and ask them if they had any distressed merchandise they would like to get out of inventory and simultaneously increase their marketing budget. Well, of course, almost every manufacturing company on earth has things sitting in warehouses or storage facilities that didn't sell as well as expected, for one reason or another. Maybe the products had a design flaw that made them fail, break or malfunction sooner than expected. Maybe the market shifted and some products were suddenly no longer sought after. Maybe Federal or state laws shifted and made the products marginally legal, or illegal or unsafe. Maybe the focus groups got it wrong and the product was never liked or desired by buyers in the first place. Maybe it was learned after the product was produced in volume and distributed to wholesalers and retailers that the product was toxic, or a choking hazard, or it had to be recalled for a serious design flaw, or it burst into flames on a hot summer day.

Many, many companies, large, medium and small, had been sitting on such distressed merchandise and wishing it would go away. The product manager wanted these products to go away because they make him look bad. The Director of R&D might look bad because his team may have developed these products. The marketing and advertising people worked hard and spent a lot of money trying to sell these dogs. Manufacturing put a lot of time and money into making the damn things. And now they have to store them in a facility somewhere and pay for that, transportation, insurance and security, and everyone wants these clunkers to just go away. So along comes Media Bartering Services and offers to take these lemons off their hands at distributers' wholesale, or whatever price was fair. MBS didn't negotiate hard to keep this number low, because, well, you'll see.

So let's take an actual case to follow the deal. A major American manufacturer and wholesaler had a subsidiary that made and distributed a million pairs of kids' one-piece pajamas. They were soft and gentle to the touch, and were touted as fire resistant. Well, sure, no one wants their kid to catch fire. So one of the salespeople was out in the field demonstrating to a retail chain buyer how fire resistant the pajamas were by holding a lighter close to the pants cuff, and the thing burst into flames like a gas-soaked sheet of newspaper. Oops, what the hell was that? Must have been one anomalous pair of pajamas. So they tested others from other batches, and you guessed it, they were all as flammable as a house of cards soaked in lighter fuel.

CEO Orca of MBS asked the product manager of the combustible pajamas to write a price on a piece of paper that he would like to get for his entire run of distressed pajamas. Orca looked at the number and said, "Fine." We'll take these schmatas off your hands for this price, but we don't pay cash, we pay you in advertising media credits. That's at book rate, of course. You are free to spend your media credits in TV or radio spots anywhere, or in print or outdoor, or any other media you desire. Well, the product manager was happy as a pig in mud.

Finally to be getting rid of these scary rags. The marketing and ad guys were thrilled to pieces because their budgets were suddenly going to be extended. The bean counters were happy because they were tired of the costs of storing these warehouses full of flame-prone pajamas. No one could see anything wrong with this deal. The legal department of Pajamas-R-Us said that they needed to have all the labels with their company name on them removed from the merchandise, and said that MBS would be restricted to selling the pajamas only in third and fourth world nations. Orca said no problem. Evidently no one was worried about the risk to third and fourth-world kids. They're just gonna be thrilled to have any pair of pajamas, which they will be using as regular clothes anyway. And their parents won't know how to complain or who to complain to when their kid's clothes keep catching fire, so to hell with them. Plus, they're living in some backwash horseshit country so they won't be able to sue.

MBS never took delivery of any of the distressed products they acquired. They were shipped immediately to a wholesaler, distributer or odd-jobber somewhere in the world who would take them to resell, sometimes at a loss to MBS, but that didn't matter. The price was no big deal, because this was not where MBS's main profits were generated.

Four things were making money for MBS. 1. The media efficiency buy. 2. The float. 3. The back-end blend. And 4. the walk-away. Let me explain:

Number one. All media is sold at a book rate. That is, there is a price list for every kind of media, what it is, where it appears, when and how often. But for a tough NYC media buying service, the book rate is only a starting point. Buyers know that there is a lot of flexibility and that sellers want to sell as much as they can; every bit of time and space available. On TV, it ranges from top prices for a prime spot in the middle of the Super Bowl, to the bottom of the barrel prices for 3:00 AM wild spots on the crappiest networks, markets and stations. The same ranges apply to radio, cable, print, and every other form of media. A good negotiator for a company that buys a lot of media can average an efficiency buy for half of the book prices. MBS buyers got that average buy down to as low as 22%! Now you remember that MBS is charging their clients the full 100% book rates, so that huge margin is the first and biggest cash generator.

Number two is the float. That's the amount of time that any company can hold on to your money, and invest it or do what they want with it, until you want to use it, or want it back. Big companies all have floats, which are for example created when you bill them for merchandise or services delivered, and they don't pay you for 90 days or more. The money that MBS made for selling the distressed merchandise goes into an offshore basket of funds making money for them in short and longer term investments.

Number three is the "back-end blend." This is something that MBS would not tell their clients about when the initial deal was struck. Here's how it worked: When Pajamas R Us would ask to expend some of its media credits to buy a saturation TV campaign in prime time in the New England market, MBS would tell them that it was unable to make the buys ordered by PRS, and that to make that happen PRS would have to add one dollar of hard cash to every media credit dollar. This was the back-end blend. Of course it was crazy and unfair, and didn't even make sense, but PRS would pay the additional 50%, in cash, to get what they wanted. They figured, hey, they were still ahead of the game because their distressed merchandise was paying for half the media costs. What they didn't realize was that the back-end cash was paying for the *entire* media buy, and if you remember that MBS was buying the media at aa low as 22% below book rate, as much as 79% of the media credit was going right into MBS profits.

Number four income source was the walk-away. Many of MBS's clients would get so frustrated and pissed off at how they were treated, and didn't dare sue because they didn't want the bad publicity generated by making flame-prone pajamas, and how they dealt with the problem by removing the labels and agreeing that their distressed merchandise could be sold to third and fourth world countries, that they would just walk away in disgust and leave whatever media credits were left on the table.

Wait, there's more. When push came to shove for some clients and they demanded to get some of their media credits back in actual money, MBS would instead offer them other deals, like outdoor media in a market they were in, or grocery cart ads, or crappy radio spots, or display print ads in papers that were hanging on for dear life. MBS's iron-clad credo was to **never pay anybody actual money for anything**. So when it came time to pay for the grocery cart ads, they would offer them some other kind of media or barter in lieu of cash. How would you like a truck full of paper party-favors, or orange juice about to expire, or ads on signs around a dog-track? Whatever, as long as it wasn't cash.

Meanwhile, the IRS had no idea how this was working, or how to collect their fair share, or tax this operation, because it was new and complicated and the books didn't show those big, fat offshore deposits in baskets of foreign currencies, and the other media deals were so weird and complex, it was many long years before the IRS could figure out how to tax corporate barter companies. And the Federal government, the regulators, didn't understand how it worked and had no idea how to regulate the new and improved corporate barter business for a long, long time. MBS was in business for nearly 20 years.

MBS made many, many millions of dollars. I just checked the Internet to see what became of them, and they are gone, gone, gone. I guess word of mouth got out, and companies with distressed merchandise just sucked it up, cut their losses, and sold the stuff to odd-lot buyers for whatever they could get. Believe me, they were better off for it. Also, the IRS finally figured out how it worked, and began to come up with ways to tax barter earnings.

Since MBS was dancing right along the edge of legality with everything they did, they had a business attorney in house or on call at all times. Jack or Orca would call the lawyer into their offices with a new scheme or idea and ask him, "Is it illegal?" And if the lawyer said yes, or probably, they would ask him, "What's our exposure?" and then, "What's the chance someone would sue us?" and then, "Could they win?"

I saw the list of clients MBS had in the mid-70's, and it included virtually every major company you ever heard of. In the engagement phase of the relationship between MBS and its client, everything looked positive and brilliant, soft and fuzzy. To turn a bunch of distressed merchandise into marketing muscle, it was a lucky blessing that fell from the sky like manna. In the honeymoon phase, after the contracts were signed, and MBS took the merchandise off their clients' hands and shipped them off to jobbers around the world (whose names were not revealed) things still looked rosy. Sometimes MBS couldn't find anyone who wanted the junk, and then they would actually sell the stuff back to the original manufacturer or distributor at an inviting discount. But as time went on, and the clients began to learn that they weren't going to get the media they wanted when they wanted it, things began to turn sour.

Almost all of MBS's clients were embarrassed that they had made or sold the products in question (like squirt-guns that leaked, digital watches that died after 90 days, electronics that were toast a few weeks after you bought them), and didn't want any press on those products or how they were sold and to whom. Initially the clients just wanted their distressed merchandise to disappear, and before long they wanted MBS to disappear. But that wasn't going to happen. This relationship was going to drag on until the client's pain was just too unbearable, and they would ask for a divorce, or just walk away. I ran into the CEO of the major company that owned Pajamas-R-Us near the end of their relationship with MBS, and he told me, fiercely and with animosity, "We hate them!"

Shafted

At one point near the end of MBS's astonishing run, a prominent New York marketing magazine interviewed Jack and Orca, and they quoted Jack as saying about MBS's clients, "We are the fuckers and they are the fuckees." By then Jack had so much money he didn't care what he said, or what his clients felt. How much money had Jack and Orca made? Well, Jack's fifth wife, who he married when he was 72, was 23 and a stunning tall blonde blue-eyed model with a body designed by angels in heaven. She liked to swim, skinny, and she didn't want to swim with the other owners in the pool on the top of their luxury Manhattan co-op building. So Jack bought the co-op below them so he could have a nice, private, in-ground pool installed in his unit. Okay, you say that's not enough. The 23 year old model wanted to be the head of a cosmetics company, so Jack bought her one, and made her the CEO.

As for Orca, he bought the mansion in Bedford Hills, NY that is now owned by George Soros. And Orca then syndicated a number of race-horses which he stabled in an equestrian facility he built next to his property. And of course, he had his own stunning blonde blue-eyed trophy wife. Her engagement diamond looked like a glass door-knob.

CHAPTER 18   WOULD YOU KNOWINGLY SELL A TOXIC PRODUCT

In the mid-seventies my NY production company was producing videos and public relations news-films for BigHair (fictional name for a huge US haircare and coloring company). After several years of servicing this client, and making good money doing it they started to think of me as one of the team, and didn't think twice about asking me to take a crew out to North Bumblewhat, New Jersey to shoot footage of their animal testing lab there. This footage would never be telecast, but would be intercut with other material (by some other company) and be used in meetings with FDA regulators in Washington, and possibly with major investors or investment advisors. The lab dealt with a side of BigHair that consumers know nothing about, and may not want to know much more than that – here's why:

People who color their hair like to believe that their skin acts as a barrier, and keeps chemicals and their potentially dangerous effects outside their bloodstream. All consumers want is to color their hair; to cover the gray and thereby keep their spouse from wandering, win friends and influence people, charm clients more easily, and create the general impression of being younger than they actually are.

These consumers may have learned in high school or college, or from watching a science program on the tube or the Web that almost every substance you put on your skin is absorbed to some degree into your bloodstream through osmosis. How much of the substance gets into your bloodstream depends on the substance, on your skin, what else is on your skin, and how long you leave it on your skin. All companies that produce products that you must handle, touch, or apply to your skin spend lots of time and money studying the effects of their products, the amount that is absorbed over X period of time, when it will make you sick, and when it will kill you.

The level of the active ingredient in a product, and the time it takes that ingredient to kill you is called the LD, or lethal dose. The period of time of application most intensely studied for each product is the average time that a consumer is likely to have contact with that product, or apply it to their skin. For example, if you produced deodorant, you would want to study the effect of your chemistry on human skin over a period of twenty four hours. Since most Americans tend to do a new application of deodorant after every shower or bath, it would make sense to test the product with a similar incidence of use.

A lab will also get results faster if they extend the exposure over time, and/or extend the potency of the solution of active ingredients.

In your hypothetical health and beauty firm, your staff scientists would want to test human subjects, but your accountants would point out that testing humans is very expensive, and there is a much greater risk of lawsuits, etc. People don't like being used as guinea pigs without their knowledge, and they rarely enjoy being disabled, crippled, rendered insane, or killed by substance testing. So it makes much more sense to set up a program to test your product on various lab animals: mice, rats, rabbits, dogs, and monkeys. These creatures can't complain, hire attorneys, or call the media. You would wisely have some out-of-state sub-contractor conduct this testing, or you would do it quietly in a nondescript building in the middle of North Bumblefuck, New Jersey, as BigHair was doing.

Here's how it works. The skins of various animals have varying degrees of osmosis, and each species' osmotic absorption rate must be measured and profiled against human osmosis for your findings to be useful. In other words, first you must find out what is different, and what is similar about the function of mouse skin to human skin before you run a zillion osmosis tests on mice. Animal hair is going to mess up the test, because most humans don't have animal hair, although there's this guy at my gym...

So the first thing you have to do to your lab animal is shave clean the area you're going to test. That would be its back, since that's the easiest to apply chemicals to, and hardest for the animal to nibble at and mess with. And this applies to all your animals, of course. You have to shave the backs of every mouse, rat, rabbit, dog and monkey. Then you have to mix up batches at various strengths of the ingredients you ask people to apply to themselves, and you have to apply those solutions to the backs of your lab animals. You can start at one end of the scale, with your ingredients at full strength, or at the other, with perhaps only a fraction of a percent of active ingredient. And you would set up a range of the various times you left the substance on the animal.

Let's say you start with full-strength 100% active ingredient, and you leave it on the animal for as long as it takes to kill it, let's say twelve hours. Well, now you know that at 12 hours, your LD is 100. If you cut the ingredient to a 50% solution, but it's still killing the animal in 12 hours, you have an LD of 50. If you reduce the time to ten minutes, which would make sense for a company that makes hair-coloring formulas, you can set ten minutes as the target time, and find your various LDs for that amount of time. Your goal here is to find what chemistry will deliver performance to the consumer at an acceptable LD.

Yes, that's right, boys and girls, there is an "acceptable" LD –acceptable to the organization manufacturing and marketing the product. Pharmaceutical companies, health and beauty companies, any company that makes anything you ingest or apply to your skin goes through this testing on an ongoing basis. Oh, yes, curious campers, I felt sorry for the poor little lab animals, too. But consider this: would you rather die, or have someone you love die because they used a particular cologne, or moisturizer, or drug, or hair color, or nail polish... or would you rather a lab in East Ratsass, New Jersey used a few lab animals to find out which substances are dangerous, and fix the problem, or made it so minuscule as to be negligible?

The fact that you're stopping for a moment to ponder the question leads us into the story that the BigHair chemists related to me over lunch:

In the mid-sixties, the FDA went to BigHair and said, hey, we hired some independent labs to test approved FDA colors, the ones you happen to be using in your products, and the labs say they show clear signs of being carcinogenic – so you've got to pull all your product off retail shelves all across the country, pronto. BigHair was using FDA reds and yellows in their formulas, as was virtually everyone else in the business.

Key executives from BigHair, and a few of their best chemists worked long days and nights to respond, then rushed to DC for a top-level meeting with the FDA regulators. BigHair and its chemists put on a show-and-tell of what American women had been doing to color and blonde their hair before BigHair. Women had poisoned themselves, scarred themselves, burned themselves, and blinded themselves with the home-brew concoctions they had produced, or grandma showed them how to make. Women were using laundry bleach, lye, tannic acid, acetic acid, paint, shoe polish, stain, roots, liniment, berries, lemon juice, beer, wine, muriatic acid, animal blood, turpentine, peroxide, intense lights, iodine, bark dies, fabric colors, Easter egg dies, vegetable extracts, tar coal, rust, artist's pigments, lead, arsenic, and other toxic and caustic substances to color their hair and cover their gray. And since it was so hard to get the color right the first time, women were going through the process twice, three times, or whatever it took to get it right, or go bald trying.

The chemists at BigHair told me that when you apply a liquid chemical to human skin for ten minutes, a surprisingly large percentage of the active ingredients or toxins gets into the bloodstream via osmosis. Which means that you have to "cut" or dilute the dangerous substances a lot before you offer your hair-coloring product to consumers. The chemists pointed out that virtually everything we eat, take or apply to our skin, if left on long enough, or used in a strong enough form, will have some toxic effect, or can be shown to be carcinogenic at some level.

For example, if you apply plain milk to the back of a mouse twenty four hours a day, every day, over a long period of time, the mouse is likely to get sick. Either that, or turn into a piece of cheese and become very popular with all the other mice.

Every company that makes and sells something that can be remotely dangerous to human health and wellbeing must factor in its LD, one way or another, and try to find a compromise between profit and freedom from lawsuits, between growth and ethics. Recall for a moment the three decade fight the tobacco industry gave the federal government on the dangers of tobacco use. Remember the fight Detroit gave the feds on the issue of seat-belts, on catalytic converters for exhaust emissions, and then on the issue of air-bags.

In each case, all the tests showed that seat-belts, catalytic converters, and air-bags would save lives, either in the short term, or the long. But the car companies were looking at how much it cost to install such things, and what it would add to the cost and the sticker price, and how they might lose market because someone else would offer a car without belts and grab that customer. Seat belts and catalytic converters had to be made mandatory, across the industry.

So, in a word, when the FDA brought BigHair in and threatened pulling product off the shelves, BigHair showed them that the alternatives were worse than anything they marketed. The chemists told me that BigHair then asked for some period of time, It was two or three years, to come up with a whole new chemistry; one with virtually no dangerous substances – and proposed marketing products with the current chemistry until they could be replaced. And the feds agreed.

The transition to the new chemicals was transparent to the consumer, and BigHair was permitted to continue to do business as usual. A compromise? Yes, of course, but one that intelligently recognized the power of vanity, and did what had to be done for the health and welfare of the greatest number of people. Can you imagine what would have happened if the hair coloring products of BigHair and all of the hair coloring and blonding products were suddenly pulled from retail shelves everywhere?

The Mob would have promptly set up undercover labs all across the country, and started churning out black-market hair color. Foreign hair-coloring products would be smuggled across borders, or concealed in antiques, souvenirs, or disguised as liquor, wood stain, or hot sauce. The cost of an ounce of Golden Blonde Medium would have risen to rapacious heights. Women would drive into scary neighborhoods at two in the morning and stop in alleyways to score their favorite color from characters with black leather jackets, guns, tattoos and pierced body parts.

Yes, I felt sorry for the helpless little animals. And I've heard the argument that they're bred for the lab, and don't know any better, and die painlessly, etc. But that doesn't help when you walk into a room full of beagles, lab beagles with nearly albino eyes, and their typical beagle markings so faint you have to squint to make them out. The lab beagles still know they're fundamentally beagles, and something in them still wants to get out of the small steel cage and chase a fox across the countryside. The lab beagles, their backs shaved and slathered with red dye, look at you just as appealingly as the puppies in the pet shop on the corner, or the captive dogs in the dog-catcher jail, and you want to ask the lab technician how much to buy all the dogs in the lab and let them go. But then you're told by the lab techs that these beagles wouldn't be able to survive on the outside. Their eyes couldn't handle the light, and their unsullied immune systems couldn't handle the bacteria and viruses of the real world. So you shake your head in resignation and move on to the next shot.

My cameraman and I went into a sterile concrete and windowless vault that was at least a hundred feet long and thirty feet wide. Four rows of shelves ran the length of the room, and each shelf carried dozens of small bins, about the size of shoe-boxes. In each bin were about ten white mice with pink eyes. Lab mice, bred for their short and miserable lives on this planet. The scientist who was showing us around the various locations had to go back to his office to get a key he forgot, and my cameraman and I were left for a couple of minutes in the long vault with the 50,000 mice.

All of a sudden this one small mouse darts across the floor and races along the edge of the wall until he comes to a door marked "ALARMED! Emergency Exit Only." That was it for Mr. Mouse – there was nowhere else to go. The poor little guy, who had been clever and athletic enough to escape his bin and shelf, would only have these few yards of freedom, these few seconds before he would be apprehended by some technician or custodial person, and probably tossed in the incinerator, since it would take hours if not days to figure out which bin he got out of. And even if he could escape, where would he go? Would he be able to survive in the real world, with his albino eyes lack of street smarts, and virgin immune system? I decided that if this one little guy was able to distinguish himself from his 49,999 peers, he deserved something better than a quick trip to the incinerator. He had made Achilles' choice, and all he needed now was some passing giant to help him take his shot.

I pushed open the bar to the alarmed door. No alarm rang. Daylight streamed in through the opening, and even though it was facing north and wasn't direct sunlight, it was stunning compared to the neon light in the lab. The rogue mouse staggered back with the power of it, and I saw his little eyelids squint. He had never seen daylight before. He pulled back a few hops and considered. He looked back into the orderly long rows of mouse bins and 99,998 little albino eyes watching him intensely. He looked up at me and my cameraman. We urged him to go for it – and suddenly he was gone. He darted out of sight under a stack of debris, wood and roofing materials next to the building. He was out there, free in the world, for better or worse.

"Yeah," said my cameraman, an unstable man whose apartment was full of Siamese cats. "Let's let 'em all go!" But that would have been excessive. And ultimately counterproductive: more than half the women in my office, not to mention my wife and mother, all used BigHair products.

I shot that footage in the BigHair lab in Jersey many decades ago, and I'm sure it's been shut down by now, or moved out of the country, or changed in response to regulatory policy, or been replaced by outsourcing to cheaper foreign nations by now, so don't write angry letters of protest to me, or my publisher, please.

CHAPTER 19 THE POT OF GOLD AT THE END OF THE RAINBOW

A few years ago in my town of Stamford, Connecticut, there was the Excelsior Hardware Company, an established older firm with some 80-100 employees. It had been around since its founding in 1910. It was started by the Mix family of New Haven, CT, to whom I am related. Excelsior's main product was locks, so in Stamford they were competing with Yale & Towne, a much larger manufacturer of locks. There was, of course, an Excelsior Hardware pension fund.

The last CEO, Robert G. Thompson, who had served in the position of president since 1986, had been dipping into the pension fund over time and virtually emptied it. Thompson had forged checks to withdraw company pension money to buy, wait for it...lottery tickets! After the missing pension funds were discovered, a company storage area was found to be filled with hidden bundles of the losing tickets, When loaded in a truck for final disposal, these tickets weighed over 480 pounds (about 800 tickets to the pound), representing a loss of hundreds of thousands of dollars.

This sad tale became a front-page story when an Excelsior employee of 65, who was retiring, filed for his pension and was told that there would be no pension, because the CEO had just been arrested for emptying out the pension fund. The distraught employee, worrying that he would be unable to support his wife and himself without the pension, shot and killed his wife and then shot himself, but he didn't die. After some time in a coma, he ended up in a state mental institution, where he did eventually succeed at dying.

In the words of a document prepared for use in the subsequent court proceedings, "In New Haven Federal Court in April, 1992, Robert G. Thompson was sentenced to serve three years for the theft of $600,000.00 from the Pension Plan. He was released in late 1994 and at this time (September 2002) continues to live in Darien, CT and is employed by a Stamford company." He was back home before he could even feel sorry for what he had done, if he ever actually did.

Excelsior Hardware Company closed in 1994, bankrupt, and with some six million dollars in debt.

CHAPTER 20 IT'S OK TO DO BUSINESS WITH WISEGUYS

A friend of a friend gave me a solid lead to a piece of new business. It was a fast-growing weight-loss franchise that was ready for some TV exposure. Let's call it "Weight-away." The tip came from a guy at an ad agency who had done some print work for the company, so my first question was why wasn't the agency doing the TV themselves? They said it wasn't profitable for them to do the media buy for a small, regional account. But I could certainly make money on the production end, couldn't I?

The agency didn't want to do the creative for the spot, either, which was fine with me, as it was another area with profit potential. A meeting was set up with the president and the marketing director of Weight-away.

The offices of Weight-away were in a second-rate two-story wood-frame building that might have previously been a storage building for a retailer of stolen wigs. No attempt had been made to make the offices look nice; everything was simply cheap and utilitarian. There was a staff of a half a dozen miserable slaves working in miserable cubicles. The boss was in one large room in front, with all the windows. His chief admin, a nervous-looking dark-haired woman of about forty, sat at a cluttered desk outside the president's office. She introduced herself as the Director of Advertising, PR and Stuff Like That.

She took me and my assistant producer in to meet the boss.

The boss was a barrel-chested man in his fifties with a one week skraggely beard and jail-house tattoos. He was, in a word, a heavy. He was hollering at someone on the phone, and using the most appalling language, when we entered. The secretary/advertising director gestured for us to sit, which we did, on a threadbare sofa that looked like it had been rescued from a local dump. I watched and listened as the president of Weight-away reduced the person on the phone to a vestige of his former self.

"I carried you for ten months, you miserable fuck," bellowed the president, "longer than your mother, you useless bum, you fucking deadbeat. So here's what's gonna happen. You bring me my fucking cash the day after tomorrow, or you're dead. You got that? Is there any fucking part of that you don't understand, you fucking deadbeat dick-faced cockroach?"

After he hung up, we were introduced to Mr. Stalicky. He offered a huge, hairy hand and vice-like grip. The stab wound in his neck, which he made no effort to conceal, probably was to blame for the gravelly voice, which made George C. Scott sound like a neutered choir boy.

"Kenny," he grated, "I've seen a coupla your spots on the tube. I like them. You come highly recommended. But I don't think I can afford your ass."

"Well, let's see what you need, Mr. Stalicky. Maybe you can and maybe you can't."

"Ha ha ha," growled Stalicky, "I like that. The kid has spunk."

We talked for a while. I learned that Mr. Stalicky was a professional usurer. His rates were five for six per week. That's five dollars loaned for six dollars to pay back at the end of one week. That's a vigorish, or "vig" of one dollar, which is twenty percent, which isn't much more than many credit cards charge on overdue debt. The only things that were different about Mr. Stalicky's credit and Visa's credit was the time span until a payment became due. With Visa, you had thirty days, and it wasn't so bad if you missed a payment, because your debt was spread over time, and you could always hold them at bay by making a partial payment. With Mr. Stalicky, the time for payment was ONE WEEK later, and if you missed that payment, the same vig was applied to the next week, and so on, until you owed Mr. Stalicky a lot of money in a very short time.

There were differences in collection procedures between Visa and Mr. Stalicky, as well. If you don't pay Visa for a while, they start with the warning letters and then calls, and eventually turn your account over to a collection agency. If you keep on not paying, they destroy your credit rating, and your name goes out on the credit bureau feeds to anyone and everyone who's running a credit check on you, and you'll have a hell of a time for years if you let it go this far.

With Mr. Stalicky, if you miss a few weeks, he makes a coupla calls to see what your problem is, and you better have a good excuse. He'll "carry you" for as long as he thinks you have the capacity to pay, eventually, because he's making money every week. However, his gut feeling about your capacity to pay will eventually cross the line formed by your rising debt, and at that point the calls will change in tone. You learn that if you don't cough up the full amount in a few days you will have your nose broken, your eyes blackened, and a rib or two snapped. If you persist in not disbursing your obligation, you will have another accident, this one more serious. Surgery, plastic surgery and bone-setting will be required. Or another avenue will be pursued. If you have some valuable property, like your business, Mr. Salicky will let you give it to him in lieu of your life. Or, maybe your new Mercedes will do the trick. Or your house. Or your first-born son will take a job for no pay. Or your pretty daughter will perform undefined services. I learned, for example, that the secretary/advertising director was the wife of man who had defaulted on a loan, and his poor spouse was keeping him alive by working for Mr. Salicky for free. The debt stayed in place, but the vig was not applied as long as the wife stayed in her full-time role as company slave.

What Mr. Stalicky wanted from me was to create and produce a TV spot for Weight-away, a company that he had garnered from the founder of the company for overdue debt. The Hungarian scientist who had invented the Weight-away system was glad to turn over his company to Mr. Stalicky instead of one more severe beating, or the disappearance of his wife and children. I didn't know this at the time, ladies and gentlemen, or I assure you I would have been out the door and speeding away in my car faster than you could open a switch-blade or snap one of my patellas.

Mr. Stalicky explained that he had found a media service that would be buying the air time, and I should coordinate with them on what they needed and when the first air date was. Stalicky wanted to do something of a saturation of the NY-NJ-CT area, and on all three major networks, but he didn't want to pay any book rates; he wanted deals, and this hoopty-scoop media service had promised him terrific deals.

So, I explained to Mr. Stalicky how TV commercial production worked: how we went back to our offices and developed ideas and scripted them and rough-boarded them and then presented them to him for his approval. I told him that I would present a production budget along with the proposal, and that if he greenlighted the project, the billing would come in three installments; one up front, one in the middle and one when the approved job was delivered to him or his media service. Mr. Stalicky had a few questions, but he understood and agreed to the process.

We went to the nearest Weight-away salon, which was in the next building, and were given a demonstration of the

Weight-away technique, which involved wrapping your pudgy body with long strips of linen, like a mummy. Where you wanted to lose the weight the fabric was wrapped tighter. Then all of your wrapped body was soaked with the secret Weight-away solution. Then your entire body up to your head was zipped into a plastic body suit. You would sit, or lay on your back in a chaise and read magazines for a half hour to an hour. The Weight-away customer didn't actually lose much fat, it was just moved somewhere nearby in the same body. So, you might want a thinner waist, and get it, but at the expense of a fatter butt, back and hips. They could take some fat from your thighs, but give you a can that could crush a mule. But I'm not a scientist, so I kept my reservations to myself. After all, I'm just the commercial production guy, I'm not supposed to express my opinion about the efficacy of the product.

We came back with our proposal, Stalicky approved it and told us to start work. We had proposed taking a month to produce the spot. He wanted it in two weeks. I told him that was impossible, and we compromised on three weeks. The budget was forty thousand, and I told Mr. Stalicky that the first third payment of $13, 233 would be due upon his execution of the letter of agreement.

"Letter of what-the-fuck?" he growled.

"It's like a contract, but less formal. It spells out what you expect and what we expect."

"Fuck that," said Stalicky. "Didn't they tell you, I don't sign nothin. I'm a man of honor, and my word is golden, you capisch? I been in business for twenty five years with no fuggin' contracts, no letters of what-the-fuck. We shake hands and that's it."

"Gotcha," said I. And we shook hands. "I'll be sending you an invoice for the first payment this afternoon."

"Fine, you do that, kid." It made me a little nervous that Mr. Stalicky called me kid. Not that I wasn't younger than him by twenty years at least, but that there was something pejorative in it; that he wasn't taking me seriously enough. But he was enthusiastic, and I had something he wanted, and he had said he was a man of honor, so I had every expectation of delivering on time, and then being paid for our work.

My assistant and I were just about to get up and take our leave when Mr. Stalicky sent his "advertising director" (who had asked us at one point what the difference was between advertising and public relations) to get something for us. She went to a room next door and returned in thirty seconds with an envelope. She handed me the envelope. I cocked it open and saw a banded stack of wrapped cash.

"What's this?" I asked Mr. Stalicky.

"Five thou," said he.

"Five thou?" said I.

"Yeah," he said. "Front money."

"Okay," said I, "I'll apply this against the first invoice, which makes it $8,233."

"Whatever makes you happy," said Stalicky, rising, and shaking my hand in a grip that only broke one of my metacarpals.

* * *

The production was a nightmare, with Stalicky insisting we shoot on location, and use some hefty bimbo he used to boink as "the model," a role we had labeled, "the victim." The model, we were assured, had once been a Playboy centerfold. It must have been one of the issues printed on a Gutenberg press. She was utterly wrong, with her mountain of hair all up in a beehive monstrosity and over-sprayed with furniture varnish, pneumatic boobs bigger and mushier than a water balloon, egregiously collagen-inflated candy-lips and clown makeup that worked in vain to cover her tired, puffy face. I couldn't talk Stalicky out of using her, so I set everything up, put her in the shot and did a couple of dry (no film running through the gate) takes of her, then I reshot the scene with a slender stunner who happened to be my wife, who was there as my assistant director.

At the shoot, Stalicky was supposed to deliver the balance of the first payment, $8,233, already overdue, but he made some excuse, and offered instead to give me a "very valuable" Oriental rug rolled up in the waiting room. I made clear to Mr. Stalicky that the rug was not to be considered a form of payment against the invoice, or I wouldn't take the thing.

"Kenny," said Stalicky. "Take the rug."

We finished the spot and delivered it on time to the media service. My third and final check, plus the balance of the first and second ones which were way overdue, were supposed to be delivered to me from Stalicky's office on the same day. I was reluctant to deliver the duplicate master to the media service until I had the checks in my hand, or cleared by the bank, but idiocy gave way to prudence, and we sent the dupe master over to the media house, which was screaming it needed it right away.

Well, I suppose you know where this is going, folks. The checks never came from Mr. Stalicky. What happened was this: the media company, which said it had sent the script and storyboards to the network standards and practices department for approval had actually neglected to do so. When they remembered that they had forgotten, they figured that if they screened the finished spot, the standards people would be more likely to accept the spot. Wrong. The spot talked about losing weight, and there was no proof that the process worked, or, more importantly, that the process was safe. No assurances from independent laboratories. No affidavits from doctors or scientists. Nothing. ABC wouldn't run the spot. NBC wouldn't run the spot. CBS said it was thinking about it, but it wanted this and that to be done, tests to be performed, etc.

The media company went back to Stalicky and offered to run the spot on cable, which had more flexible standards. A disclaimer could be added to the spot, as a super. But, no, Stalicky wanted network, the cache of network. The business was already a sleazoid operation, what they didn't need was to try and market it in second-class media (which cable was at the time).

I didn't know what had happened with the network approvals until I called Mr. Stalicky to ask why he hadn't taken care of any of the invoices as he had promised, since he had told me he was a man of honor. There was a long pause on the other end of the line. Finally Mr. Stalicky spoke:

"Kenny, I gave you five thousand clams for that piece of shit, which no one will run, so it isn't worth the film you shot it on. That's all you'll be getting. Don't call me again on this. Ever. Is that totally fuggin' clear?"

"Yes, but…"

And Mr. Stalicki hung up. I called my attorney, Jack Scherer, and asked him what I should do.

"You made a TV spot for 'Two-fingers' Stalicki?" asked Jack, incredulous.

"Yes. I didn't know his name was 'Two-fingers.' He had ten fingers when I met him."

"Ken, listen, here's what you're going to do. You're going to eat the balance due and mark it up to experience. And Ken, listen: you're never going to call or mail or contact Two-fingers Stalicky about the invoices, or about any other damn thing under the sun, ever again. I'm not shittin' you. Are you hearing me?"

"But…"

"Do you like life? Do you love your wife and daughter?"

"Absolutely."

"Then, promise me."

"All right, Jesus. I promise."

"And you'll never, ever, do business again with those people, or anybody like them. What were you thinking?"

"I guess not much."

CHAPTER 21   HOW TO MAKE MILLIONS IN STOCKS ONLINE

In mid-September, 1999, Ann Rae Heinz's (fictitious name) very successful husband passed away, and left her $10 million dollars. Six million was in US treasury bonds and four million in tax-free municipal bonds and bond funds. Then there was the main house in Phoenix, worth around $2.7 million. And about a half dozen luxury cars and art and jewelry, etc.

I attended the funeral and Ann took me aside and said, "I know you have been trading stocks online, and I want to do that, too. Can you tell me what computer system I need, and what apps, and what firm to trade with?"

"Uh, sure, Ann," I said, "but why would you want to fool around with trading? You have ten million dollars cash and a mortgage-free house. Now you just kick back and rest on your laurels, travel, live well, and enjoy a stress-free life."

"Do I need to hire someone to teach me how to use the equipment and apps, or do you think I can just noodle it out myself."

"You're crazy," I said.

"I'm planning on making a million a month," she said. "At least."

"Ann, ten million in the bank is enough. Quit while you're ahead."

"Are you going to help me or not?" she said.

Ann Rae couldn't wait to get on the internet and try her hand at trading securities. Let me help you understand her enthusiasm to dive into this maelstrom of sharks.

When she was younger, in 1967, her mother died and Ann inherited some $17,000 dollars. She had no background in investing and knew basically nothing about how to handle money or invest. She signed up for a course offered by one the big investment firms in Manhattan, Merrill Lynch or Bache & Co, I forget. I don't know if she completed the course, as she had a propensity for not finishing things, like junior college, a sewing course, a cooking course, etc.. But in that investing course one of her classmates was this "sawed-off, nondescript woman" named Mickie Siebert. Mickie seemed to understand what was going on, and was picking up things quickly and thoroughly. Ann, who was drop-dead gorgeous and very popular with the men in the course, thought to herself, hey, I'm as smart as her. I can do this investment stuff, no sweat.

Soon afterwards, Ann was at a cocktail party and found herself talking to a young stock analyst. Ann asked him for a tip and he said, "Syntex. They made the first oral contraceptive pill, and there's a new hotshot President at the helm. They have a new drug about to be approved by the FDA. It's gonna be huge." So Ann put the whole $17,000 into Syntex. But a couple of bad things happened shortly after that. Searle and Company beat them out on securing FDA approval of the new drug Syntex was banking on. And then Syntex's submission of a fraudulent toxicology analysis of naproxen led to the <u>Food and Drug Administration</u>'s uncovering extensive scientific misconduct on the part of the lab. The stock took a bath, and ultimately, the dregs of Syntex was absorbed into Searle. Ann's $17,000 investment went down the drain totally. So whenever Ann would tell her wealthy husband that she wanted to play the market, he only had to say one word to rein her in: "Syntex."

But now he was dead, and Ann had, count 'em, $10 million free dollars to play with. Yikes!

I did suggest a computer system with two big monitors, and a securities firm that had a snazzy interface, and before I got on the plane to fly back to Connecticut, Ann was receiving delivery of her shiny new computer system.

After a month I called Ann to see how she was doing. She didn't sound happy.

"I haven't told anyone else, but I didn't make a million this month. I, uh, instead, *lost* a million. Well, a little more, actually."

"Ann, listen, you don't know what you're doing. Wall Street is going to kill you. Even experienced traders often lose a bundle, and they're insiders. You're not plugged in. You're not hanging around with the right people. Stop trading, sell the computer and get the hell out of there."

A month later she called me and said, "How much do you know about shorting?"

"Oh, my God," I said. "Listen, Ann, when you choose a stock and put money in it, it's because you have been watching that stock, or you are familiar with their business and products, and you believe they are going to prosper. Shorting is the opposite of that. You watch the stock, you do a lot of research, and then you borrow the stock and sell it immediately for its current worth. Then it tanks, you buy it at the short price and return the stocks to the lender and pocket the difference."

"Wait, say that again," she said.

"Look, it's very complicated and you can lose a bunch because you will be tempted to buy on margin. You can leverage up your original dollar to *nine times* that. But if you didn't guess right, and the stock goes up instead of sinking, you can lose your shirt when there's a margin call. You can lose way more than your original investment."

"Wait, can you repeat that?"

"Listen, just don't do it, okay? You have to be a financial dweeb to even understand how it works."

"Yeah, but the talking heads on CNBC are saying that Amazon and Google and Apple can't sustain this kinda growth, and they're due for a U-turn."

"Oh my God, Ann, please, don't short anyone. Especially don't short Apple, Amazon and Google. Jesus Christ, don't listen to CNBC. Those people are on the sell-side. They're entertainers. They probably know less than you. You can't come and move in with us when you lose your shirt, okay? We don't have the room. Just don't bank on that. I'm sorry."

Several months later I got a call from Lynn (not her real name), Ann's personal secretary. Lynn was Ann's right hand, and her left hand, too. Lynn came to Ann's house every morning and stayed until dinner, or sometimes after. She ran the house, did the shopping, managed Ann's schedule, her social life, medical appointments, car maintenance, garden and grounds maintenance, wardrobe, laundry, housecleaning staff, payroll, insurance, taxes, EVERYTHING. I'm not sure Ann was safe alone in the bathroom or the kitchen without Lynn. When Lynn called me she was in Hawthorne, NY, not far from Stamford and Greenwich, CT, where I was selling residential real estate. Lynn asked me if I could recommend an agent in the Hawthorne area.

"Lynn, what are you doing in Hawthorne?" I asked.

"I have family here," she said.

"No," I said, "why aren't you in Phoenix with Ann?"

"Uh, you better talk with her about that," said Lynn."

So right after I got off the phone with Lynn I called Ann and asked what was up.

"Can you hold on for a minute?" she said. "I have this man on the line who is buying my Rolex." And she put me on hold.

After a couple of minutes she came back on. "Oh my god," she said, "I'm wiped out. Totally shafted. Every last cent. The margin call killed me. I had to sell the house and the cars. The jewelry and the art. Why didn't you warn me about the margin call?"

"I did!" I said. "But you weren't listening. You were like a kid in a candy store. A kid with a sugar obsession."

"I sold the house at a loss for $1.9, and I sold the cars, all but one. I need to drive to get places out here, you know. Apple and Google and Amazon didn't tank. They kept on kicking ass stronger than ever, and, uh hold on, there's someone calling to buy one of the big Lindermans." (Earl Linderman was a painter who was hot in Arizona at the time.) She put me on hold again, and after about seven minutes, I hung up.

I didn't talk with her for a while until Christmas rolled around. Ann and her husband used to come to NYC for the holidays and often visited super rich friends of theirs who owned the entire top floor of an upscale hotel near the Plaza. Let's call them the Freedoms. Well when Francine Freedom heard that her friend Ann had lost it all in the market and couldn't afford the air fare to visit for Christmas, she sent her a ticket and invited her to stay at their place. Ann was happy to oblige.

Francine gave a super-posh cocktail party and at that party Ann was a center of attention because she was still attractive, and was the woman who had lost it all in a year. One of the interested members of her audience was a New York attorney who was active in cases in the financial sector. He approached Ann with a proposition.

"Okay," he said, "who were you trading with?

"Merrill Lynch," said Ann.

"And who was your broker there?" said the lawyer.

Ann gave him her broker's name. The attorney didn't know it, had never heard it before.

"Listen, Ann," he said, "Here's the deal. I'll go after Merrill, and whatever I can recover, we split 50-50, okay?"

"Okay," said Ann. "Deal." And they shook hands.

"What's your email address?" he said, and Ann gave it to him.

"You'll get a contract tomorrow. Sign it, scan it and return it to my office, and we're in business."

A week and a half later Ann was back home in Phoenix. She got an email from the NY attorney who told her that they were in luck. He had done some digging and found out that the woman Ann was trading with had been a *trainee* when she did most of Ann's trades! The Merrill woman wasn't licensed to trade, boys and girls. She had picked up the phone when her boss was out and she and Ann started chatting and the next thing you knew, Ann was placing trades with her. The upshot was that Merrill settled for a million dollars. So the lawyer got half, and the other half went to Ann.

"Jesus, you're so lucky," I said.

"Yes, yes I guess I am," she said.

"If you ever buy another stock, I'll never talk to you again."

"Ha ha," said Ann.

She moved into a much less prestigious residence in Phoenix, and is living now much closer to the vest, and seems to be happy and settled. I did learn that she was still playing in the market, but just for fun now, and with much tinier investments. She wasn't shorting anyone, anywhere, ever again. She is 80 now, still seems to be mentally sharp, and I think she'll be okay for the rest of her life.

Meanwhile, Muriel "Mickie" Siebert, that "sawed-off nondescript woman" Ann met in the investing class, became the first woman to have a seat on the NY Stock Exchange, and her company Muriel Siebert & Co, is one of the top investment brokerages in the world.

CHAPTER 22 MARILYN, AN AMERICAN FABLE

I n 1981 I was living in Manhattan with my third wife, the heiress, Lin Berlitz. Her father, Charles Berlitz, was the grandson of the man who started the Berlitz language schools. But Charles had made his own fortune; he was the author of *The Bermuda Triangle*. I was operating my production company, Delmar Productions, in mid-town Manhattan, and Lin was working for me as a producer.

It may have been Lin who introduced me to Jeanne Napoli, the singer and music producer, and wife of James "Jimmy Nap" Napoli, Caporegime of the Gambino family. "Gentleman Jim" as he was also known, was doing a stretch at Danbury Federal, AKA "Club Fed", and Jeanne was making her way as a music producer in NYC. She contacted me to produce a music video for this handsome young singer from Australia. The singer couldn't sing a note, but that wasn't important because he had a rich male sponsor who was going to make him a star. The two men were living together in the Plaza Hotel.

I met with Jeanne in her handsome brownstone in the east sixties of Manhattan to discuss the video job. The rich Australian guy wanted to make his young trick a rock star as quickly as possible, and he was throwing a ton of money at the project. He had hired the best PR company for rock stars; a manager, Jeanne to put together a band and produce an album; the best stylist in town; the hot hair stylist of the month; a famous voice coach to help give the young man a voice; and a creative video guy (me) to make a music video to go with the album. It was, in a word, a travesty. But the money was good and fast, so Jeanne put together a band ("Street Fighters") and she and some friends wrote several tunes, a rehearsal space was rented and recording studio booked. I shot and produced a kickass video around the strongest tune in the album, "Street Fighters." The promotion people got the would-be rock star on guest shots and talk shows, selling him as a phenom rock star in Australia, because it was Australia so who knew?

I insisted on being paid in cash before I would deliver the finished and approved master to the rich Australian. A Manhattan bank did give me a fat envelope full of cash, and I had a great time making the video. But then the whole effort to make a star out of very thin air imploded one evening when the would-be rock star had a quickie with some guy he met in Central Park. The wanna-be star got beaten up and couldn't make several appearances, but more importantly his wealthy patron's heart was broken. Not long after the Central Park incident, he packed up and flew back to Australia.

But the good news was that I had impressed Jeanne, so that when she came up with the idea of producing a Broadway musical on the story of Marilyn Monroe, she asked me to write the libretto. In a musical, like in an opera, the libretto is the through-line, the plot and the spoken words. The lyrics and the music are written by song writers. This was a huge opportunity for me, and I dove into it with enthusiasm and focus. My dad had starred on Broadway for nine months in 1950 in a Johnny Mercer musical called "Texas Lil Darlin," so I was not unfamiliar with the environment of the Broadway musical stage. We did not discuss money because that would have been premature. But I was confident that if the show was even a minor hit, and I wrote the libretto, I would be well compensated for my creative contribution.

The key ingredient in theatrical production is money. Without that, you have no production. The next important component is the people. Then luck, and timing, and magic. Then some more money, because everything always costs more than you anticipated. And shit happens. It is also important that the people can work together. There are always large egos involved, and often oversize egos bump into one another and it takes professionalism for those egos to compromise for the sake of the show. Theater people like to work with their friends, and they work hard to bring their friends into a production that looks like it's going to make the boards, and maybe be a hit. A musical about Marilyn Monroe could be a hit. Should be a hit.

Jeanne's husband, "Gentleman Jim," started the financial ball rolling with a quarter of a million dollars. "Marilyn, An American Fable" was on its way. I did a bunch of research on her life and cobbled together a storyline. It was not a finished libretto, but did have a complete plot, a beginning, middle, and an end, and several scenes in full dialog. It gave a good sense of the story, structure and pacing. Jeanne was very happy with it and was impressed with how fast I was able to get it done. Meanwhile, several other producers had jumped into the mix, and were using their financial contribution to exercise their influence and involve their friends. The initial actress-singer that was slated to play Marilyn was tossed and replaced by Alyson Reed. Composers were piling on. First it was Jeanne and Doug Frank. Then came Gary Portnoy. Then came others until at final count there were ten composers and sixteen producers.

Jeanne invited me to her house to talk about my first draft of the libretto. I fully expected there were going to be what are called "notes," which are recommended alterations, deletions and additions made by people with clout, as in the producers and people under their control. I do have pride of authorship, but I was ready for criticism, opinions and questions of taste and dramatic structure. The minute I set foot in Jeanne's living room, she offered me a glass of very old, very expensive bourbon, which she knew was my favorite drink at the time. She served it to me in a brandy snifter with a splash of branch water and a couple of rocks, just the way I like it.

"That bad, huh?" I said.

"You need to sit, Ken."

"Good grief."

"I have lost control of my project," said Jeanne. "I am being camped to death."

"But it was your idea. And Jimmy put in a bunch of money. And..."

"They put in more money. And Jimmy is up in Danbury Federal. He doesn't want to have anything more to do with the project. He did it for me."

"So, what happened with my script?"

"Your libretto is out. You are out. I'm really sorry about this, Ken. They brought in one of their friends, of course, to write the libretto. I fought and bitched, but there it is."

"Did they even read my sides?"

"They said they did. They said it was too straight."

"They actually said it was too straight?"

"Let me give you an example. They created a character that is not one but three fey singers to represent Marilyn's three vices, drugs, liquor and sex, in over-the-top costumes. This campy trio is called Destiny, and whenever they sing they sprinkle fairy dust around."

"Do you have any air-sickness bags?"

"They put in a dance number with plumbers in pink plumbers outfits. I said absolutely not. It's still in. When I speak they ignore me. Or no, sometimes they pay attention and then make fun of me. It's a nightmare. Marilyn will be the death of me."

"I'm so sorry. But how is the show? Is the show coming together?"

"I wince through every scene. I'm worried my face is going to stick in a permanent wince. Alyson Reed, who plays Marilyn, is a pro, and she works very hard to deliver a solid, honest performance, but then they camp it up and make her trials and tribulations feel silly and slight."

"I feel bad that I'm shafted. But I feel even worse for you. What are you going to do?"

"Drink lotsa martinis. And there's always suicide."

"No. Suicide is not an option. If you commit suicide I'll... never talk to you again."

"Did I waste good bourbon on you?"

"No, I'm enjoying every drop of it."

"I do have some good news for you. Jimmy said okay to your idea of the Cosa Nostra and the Hell's Angels."

"Really?"

"I was surprised, too."

"I'm going to write it as a book."

"Oh. I thought you meant it as a screenplay."

"I did. I already wrote it as a screenplay. But nobody takes an original screenplay seriously. It has to start out as a book. Some major element takes an interest in it, someone comes up with the money, then some Hollywood screenwriter converts it into a screenplay. That's the drill."

"Well, it's your idea, so write it any way you want."

"Thanks, Jeanne, I didn't think you'd actually run it by him."

"My pleasure, Ken. And I want to pay you for the time you put into Marilyn."

"Don't be silly. I'm a big boy. And I made good money off the Australian guy."

"I just can't wait for Marilyn to die. Again."

"C'mon, it was a great idea, Jeanne. Just consider it a lesson learned. Your next show will be a hit."

"There will be no next show. I will never do this again. I will not survive this."

Jeanne was right. "Marilyn, An American Legend" was deservedly panned by Frank Rich of the Times, and only ran for 17 performances. Jeanne never produced another show. She began to suffer bouts of clinical depression, and she began getting sick, and then staying sick. Eventually she was hospitalized and died there in 2010.

CHAPTER 23   IF IT'S TOO GOOD TO BE TRUE...

A financial guy, let's call him Fatso, and a marketing guy, let's call him Peddler, got together with a great idea to make a bundle fast: they would sell one ounce gold Krugerrands for less than the government of South Africa or any bank or coin dealer in the world. I don't know what the going price was then, but the price for one Krugerrand on February 24, 2018 was $1,375.70. So they would offer to sell that coin for, say, $1,275.70, a pure and simple $100.00 discount. Wherever the price went, (it was directly linked to the price of gold) they would offer it for $100 less. It was an investor's no-brainer.

Fatso and Peddler set up a corporation in the state of Connecticut, took a small office space in Stamford, brought in a bunch of phone lines, several computers, and hired some young office personnel. They bought some twenty five Krugerrands. They initiated a relationship with an out-of-work advertising guy from NYC, who set himself up as a small local agency to service them. The NYC ad man, a friend and fellow member of my local club, was my source of information for this misadventure. The two partners put most of their front money into a nation-wide saturation ad campaign, mainly in print media. This was in the early eighties, so there was no World Wide Web as we know it today, but had there been they would have used it extensively.

The advertising didn't have to say much; just quote the low price of the fixed commodity, state that it would always be $100 below the going price, and tell potential buyers that they were limited to three coins per customer. This was to somehow offset the assumption that something was wrong with the deal, which was quite obvious to anyone with half a brain. How could a business sell Krugerrands for $100 less than they were worth at any bank or numismatist in the world? Well, you limit the sale to only three per customer and make it up in volume, that's how. People were so anxious to take advantage of the offer, they put their common sense on hold and sent money orders or certified bank checks as fast as they could. And, they cleverly got around the limit of three per customer by ordering additional coins in the name of spouses, children, siblings, dead relatives, or family pets. When I asked my friend the ad man how the two partners could make any money on this deal, he said "I don't know. They sort of explained it to me, something about shorting the asset, but it didn't make any sense so I just stopped asking."

The twenty five Krugerrands were held by Fatso, only to be forwarded when absolutely necessary to those people who called the cops, or raised a big stink. Fatso and Peddler hired more people to man the phones, process orders and handle complaints. The phones began ringing off the hooks, and mail began arriving daily in fat canvas bags. The young employees, some of them still in high school, must have seen that there was no fulfillment department. They must have learned pretty fast that no one, except the violent and vocal customers, was getting their Krugerrands. Meanwhile thousands upon thousands of orders were pouring in. All money orders or certified bank checks. Fatso and Peddler didn't allow credit cards, because there are too many consumer protections. Plus the wait to be reimbursed by the credit card company would have made it difficult to fly the coop on short notice.

I understand Fatso and Peddler were doing so well that they broke down and bought another fifty Krugerrands, to deal with the belligerent types, but that they only delivered several these coins to buy time before they absconded. The two fly-by-night businessmen grabbed the funds and left the country. It was in the original plan. The advertising guy got his final payment and dropped out of circulation. I heard that he had broken up with his wife and moved to NYC. But the kicker is that the two partners had the audacity to hang around for a while, proclaiming their innocence. Maybe they needed the time to sell and move all their assets out of the country, or more likely, they were still receiving valid money orders and certified checks.

While the state was preparing legal moves, and the city cops were entering the office space with warrants, Fatso and Peddler were crying foul, and saying that they meant to deliver all the coins ordered, but that they were just having trouble buying them and getting them into the country. They were buying time, making tens of thousands each day they could extend the caper. The story moved to the back of the paper, and my memory of its resolution has moved to the back of my mind, but in the end, I recall, one of the two partners fled to Brazil and the other one returned to the US, was prosecuted and did time. It must have been Fatso, because I recall him asking for lighter sentence because he was in poor health and had a family in Greenwich with school-age kids. The advertising guy walked away scot free by claiming that he didn't have any idea what was going on. This is a rather amazing stretch, since his office was right next door to the partners, and he was a key part of the operation. It just wasn't worth it to the authorities to go after him, I suppose. The last time I saw him I was playing tennis at my club Club and heard from the bushes at the edge of the courts a "Pssst, Hey Ken, do you wanna buy a couple of almost new computers for a song?"

Where do these three characters fit in the opinions of their peers? The one who did time, Fatso, came down a peg or two, because not only did he get caught, but he did time, and he paid a fat fine. But he is still something of a winner, because he salted a goodly sum of money away in some offshore bank, and is probably fixed for life. So, he is something of a modern hero.

The ad guy got to keep the money he made for his work handling the media placements. He probably got tired of explaining to people he knew in the community that he didn't know what was going on, honest Injun. As far as I know, he didn't get indicted, and didn't do time. But the amount of money he took off the table is hardly enough to retire on, so he is only a minor hero, temporarily, with reservations.

Peddler is a hero, a modern success, and to the people who surround him wherever he lives in Brazil, where they have no extradition treaty with the US, he is, no doubt, a respected, wealthy man. No one there knows how he got his money, and no one cares. In today's craven culture, Peddler is a winner. And what about the thousands of people across the country who took money from their hard-earned nest eggs to invest in "safe" Krugerrands – and lost a bunch? Well, it's nothing personal... it's just business.

CHAPTER 24   "ALL THE WORLD'S A STAGE"

I was operating a film production company in 1979. We had an office in Manhattan in the Time and Life building, and one in Stamford CT, in a converted barn in North Stamford. This was a tax advantage for several of our clients, because I would bill the NYC clients out of the CT firm, and the Connecticut clients out of the NY company. And just to remain a straight shooter, I did the work for our NY clients in the CT studio, and the Connecticut work in the NY City offices. Mainly. I liked working in Stamford, because that's where I lived. It was a very short commute from my house to the converted barn on the property.

Most of my important clients were in Manhattan, of course, but I did like having a few irons in the fire up in Connecticut, and nearby Westchester County. There was a small ad agency in Riverside, CT. called Kohler. And a medium-size ad agency in Rye, NY, run by two ex-NYC admen, Herb Sklar and Paul Lenett. It was called Sklar-Lenett Associates. Neither of these agencies had an in-house TV department, so they were happy to find and do business with me, as I provided not only TV production services, but performed the creative services as well.

Herb Sklar called me one morning and told me they were talking with two guys who founded and owned the Off-Off Dinner Theater (Not the real name) in Westchester County, about producing and running spots on area TV for their theatrical productions. Off-Off had a rep for putting on near-Broadway caliber productions, and the food wasn't bad, it was said. Herb and I talked about what might be involved in producing a 30 second spot of an upcoming show, how it would be done, what issues would come up with the various unions and guilds, and what it would cost. The agency, Sklar-Lenett, would take care of all disbursements, and would execute the media placements. I knew that the agency had never done anything like this, so I warned Herb to make sure he and the agency were compliant and would follow the guidelines of network Program Standards and Practices vis-à-vis any necessary clearances, releases and approvals before any air time was booked.

This was in '79, before cable TV had serious marketing momentum, so it was a matter of getting your ducks in a row with the main channels and their standards people. The product and services being offered were not any pharmaceutical edible, cosmetic, medical or dangerous product, substance or service, so getting the necessary clearances would not be a serious hurdle. The agency would have to deal with the actors who were going to appear in the show, and in the TV spot as well. They would have to pay allegiance and kneel at the stations of the cross of Actor's Equity, and also of Screen Actors Guild. My companies were signatories to all the appropriate unions and guilds, so that would save the agency having to go through those steps. I told Herb that a ball-park estimate to produce one 30 second spot, shooting on location at the theater in Elmsford and posting in NYC to an air date four days later, would be $20,000. Okay, he said, sounded reasonable to him.

About a week later I went to the site of the theater, to meet the owners, survey the location, meet and talk with some of the techs on-site, and get a free dinner as well.

At the meeting, which Herb and I attended, I met the two young guys who owned and ran the theater. Let's say their names were Tweedlebob and Tweedlebill. They were earnest, and seemed nice enough. Clearly stressed, though. Very worried about every little thing. What if this went wrong, what if that went wrong, etc. What if the performance flopped? What if my commercial sucked? How come it cost so much? They couldn't see what cost $40,000 for a few day's work on one location with one evenings shoot. I didn't blink because it wasn't my first time at the rodeo, and I knew the agency would mark the production cost up. I did think that doubling it was pushing the envelope a bit hard, as it was clear that these dinner-theater guys were not getting rich off this business. Herb jumped in quickly and said that they would look hard at the budget and sharpen their pencils as much as possible. He looked at me and I nodded that I would sharpen my pencil as well. My thought was that it was going to be a pretty simple, straightforward shoot with one location and four or five set-ups, all at the same location, and that the real pressure would come in the very tight schedule to air.

Later with Herb and Paul I agreed to produce the spot for $18,000. We were to be paid in thirds; one third up front, one third with the approval of the rough-cut, and one third when we delivered 16mm prints to them or directly to the networks. The first spot we were to produce was for the two-character comedy "Same Time Next Year," by Bernard Slade. It was starring Betsy Palmer and Tom Troupe. The play covers 25 years, the period from 1951 to'76, with the scene of the couple meeting being staged every five years. It was a popular play and ran for years on Broadway. Betsy had starred for a couple of years there, and Tom had starred in the show on the road. Betsy was a friend of my dad, and they had seen each other socially several times in Danbury, CT, where they both had houses. Betsy knew me from when I was a little kid, and I was looking forward to working with her on this TV spot. The show would go into rehearsals in three weeks, and I would come and shoot the dress rehearsal, then edit, mix and print for the networks quick like a bunny and get the release prints to them four days later. This was in the days of film, before digital video, so to get prints to the networks in three days would require sleepless nights and working around the clock to make the deadline. It would be impossible to make the deadline working entirely in film, so we were going to edit and finish in video.

I billed immediately for the first third payment and called to make sure my invoice arrived at the offices of the Elmsford

Dinner Theater. It had, and then my wife and I left for a week of skiing at Keystone in Colorado with our best friends.

We were out on the mountain about to get on the lift when the girl tending the loading area asked me if I was Ken Delmar. When I said yes, she told me there was an important phone call for me from New York. I could take the call at the ski shop. I came down off the hill and called back the number in New York. It was Herb Sklar, the guy from the ad agency.

"Ken," said Herb, "There's been an emergency. "Same Time Next Year" has been moved up two weeks. You have to come back right away and produce the spot."

"What!?" I whined. "I just got here."

"I know. I feel terrible about it, but it is what it is. Can you do it?"

"Jeez, I don't know. We have another job we're just finishing up for Clairol."

"It's too late for us to get someone else."

"I was really looking forward to this vacation."

"I know. It's terrible, but you can do it, Ken. It'll be fun."

"It won't be fun. It'll be a nightmare. Staying up all night editing. Mixing at three in the morning."

"You're young and strong."

"This'll put an end to that."

"Get on a plane. I'll pick you up at the airport. You can fly right into the Westchester County Airport."

"I bet you checked."

"Of course I checked."

"This job will kill me, Herb."

"Rolling off a log. Four days and you're done. Check yourself right into a hospital."

So I took off my ski outfit and put on my street clothes and flew home to produce the TV spot for "Same Time Next Year."

But something was bugging me. The first payment for the production, which was due the minute they asked me to produce the spot, was not forthcoming. I asked about it and Herb said something about problems with the box office. And there was some other problem with a lawsuit. But Herb said not to worry about it. He pointed out that this was theater. They had ups and downs. When they were doing shows and serving dinners the cash was coming in. When they were between shows, cash was flowing out. One season dinner theater was hot and the next season not. Once the show was up and running, the cash would be pouring in.

Herb came into NYC and to our offices to look at the rough cut, which he loved and approved. After the screening we stopped by a nearby joint to talk. I brought up the fact that I had not yet seen the first-third payment on the production.

"I feel your pain," said Herb. "We haven't gotten a nickel from them either. They keep reassuring us that we just have to be patient. They say this is how it is in theater. Broadway, the East End, Off-Broadway, it's all the same."

All my expenses are coming in hot and heavy on this short runway. Rawstock, crew and staff, processing, mixing, transfers, titles, dubs, it's all going to hit in one week, overtime and triple-turn-around time, and I'm going to be paying it all out of pocket."

"Listen," he said, "Paul and talked about it and we sort of felt like middlemen. I mean, like, you're doing all the work. The creative, and everything, and we're just sort of playing Mike in The Middle. We're thinking it makes more sense just to put you together directly with the owners. Like you cut a new contract between you and them. It's no skin off their nose. And they keep whining about the cost, so working with you directly they'll save our markup. All the terms would be the same, just you and they are the two parties."

"I could do that."

"Yeah, except for the media buy. We will still do the media placement."

"Sounds like a plan."

"With such a short runway, it'll help streamline the process."

"Absolutely."

So that's what we did. I wrote a contract that night between my company and the two guys from the dinner theater, Tweedlebob and Tweedlebill, and had it delivered to them the next day, after we all talked about it on the phone. No one had any problems with the deal. They promised to sign it and fax it back the next morning, but that didn't happen. Normally I would have checked these guys out on Dun & Bradstreet, and vetted them to make sure they were straight shooters, but there was no time, and Sklar-Lenett said they had vetted them anyway. We had an air date four days after the shoot. It was an insane job, fraught with colossal stress, and the only way I could do it was because I was young, strong and insane.

We finished the job, made a few dubs and rush messengered them to the NY area stations just in time for air. Everyone was happy and amazed. I crashed and fell asleep on the sofa in my office. I slept about twelve hours. When I woke up my cameraman was poking me in the shoulder.

"Hey, wake up," he said. "Herb is on the phone. He told me to wake you up. So, get up." I got up, sat at my desk and picked up the phone to talk with Herb.

"Ken, are you sitting down?"

"You mean, I'd better be sitting down?"

"That's right. I have not good news for you. And for us. Bad news enough for everyone."

"I'm too weak and numb for bad news, Herb."

"Tweedlebob and Tweedlebill are bankrupt. Our attorney called a few minutes ago with the news."

"Bankrupt? But doesn't it take weeks to go bankrupt. Months... they just went bankrupt in the last few hours?"

Well, it's even worse than bankrupt. They're insolvent. There's no money in the till. Nada, zippo, butkus. No twenty five cents on the dollar. No nothing. Casters up. Final curtain."

"You're serious."

"As serious as an open-casket funeral."

"But the spots are running right now, as we speak."

"That's right, on our dime."

"Can't you stop them?"

"We booked the air. We're on the hook, unless we go bankrupt as well, and we're not going to do that."

"Jesus Christ."

"We have a meeting with our attorney in a half hour. He'll do what he can to stop the bleeding, but this is going to knock the wind out of our sails no matter what."

"You have to sue them. I have to sue them."

"Good luck with that. Our attorney says you can't squeeze blood from a stone."

"But... But... But..."

"Ken, it's a corporation. They're insolvent. Not a shekel in the till. We would have to prove intent to defraud and even then it wouldn't make any difference, they have the protection of the corporate veil. We can't touch their personal money or property."

"But we have bills coming in right now, and more on the way, and so do you. This isn't fair. This can't be right."

"Who said the law is fair? Who said the law is right? It's like Shakespeare said, 'The law is an ass.'"

"Wait, that was Dickens."

"Well, they're both right."

Postscript: I just went on the Internet (Feb 5, 2020) to see if the Off-Off Dinner theater had risen from the ashes, and there it was, full steam ahead, under a new name, of course, but still owned and run by Tweedlebob and Tweedlebill. Yes, it's legal. It's corporate law, ladies and gentlemen. Tweedlebob and Tweedlebill didn't even have the decency to invite me to a complementary dinner and a show. Probably worried that I would have punched them in their respective noses.

EPILOG

It's sad to me that our country, and maybe the whole "civilized" world, has slid down the slippery slope to a place where you really need, more than ever, a Dutch uncle or aunt, or a book like *Shafted, Cautionary Tales in Business*, to help prepare you for the hazards, pitfalls, villains, obstacles, betrayals, setbacks, changes of fortune, and slings and arrows that inevitably lie ahead.

If this book has helped arm you for one or more assaults, , and helps you anticipate or spot such hurdles and antagonists early on, avoid them or beat them, and, when possible, serve evil-doers their just desserts, all Dutch uncles and aunts everywhere will celebrate and do a little jig. If you listen carefully you may hear us dancing.

ABOUT THE AUTHOR

KEN DELMAR, author, fine artist, playwright, sailor, kayaker, and registered Dutch Uncle; formerly a producer/director/writer, was the head of a successful film/video production company from 1970 till 2000. He grew up in Manhattan and Los Angeles, attended Trinity School (NYC), Middlebury College (BA '63), and Columbia University. He is or was a member of the Dramatists Guild, the Authors Guild, the Screen Actors Guild, the Connecticut Association of Realtors, and the Stamford Yacht Club.

In 1968, after serving two years in the US Army during the Vietnam War, he returned to the USA with a soon-to-be pregnant wife and $137. He started Delmar Productions in a Stamford, Connecticut barn he shared with a family of raccoons, a couple of possums and several swallows. Within five years, he had offices in the Time & Life Building in Rockefeller Center, a home of his own on the Connecticut shore with a beach, a new Mercedes, a twenty-eight-foot sloop, membership in a yacht club, and an income in six figures when that meant something. He lives with his wife and daughter in Stamford, Connecticut, where they are selling residential real estate as Delmar Group at Keller Williams, and Ken is writing compelling books like *Winning Moves, Body Language for Business; No Fall Zone, Fall Prevention and How to Fall if You Do;* and *Shafted, Cautionary Tales in Business.*

If you enjoyed this book, or gleaned something from it that will help you anticipate obstacles and achieve your goals, please write a short review and send it to Amazon, or any other book review site, and thanks a lot for that!

KenDelmarAuthor.com
khdelmar@gmail.com

www.ingramcontent.com/pod-product-compliance
Lightning Source LLC
Chambersburg PA
CBHW051753040426
42446CB00007B/353